She woke early.   Refreshed, no; content, maybe. The nightmares, that were a constant reminder of just how close she had come to dying on that mountainside, were finally starting to lessen in their intensity and frequency, and for that, she was thankful. The thin scars on her wrists were fading and were the last visible reminders of what had happened to her that day, less than a month ago. The bruises had long since healed and life at the lodge, for the most part, had returned to normal. She had agreed to stay on to help the owners, Andrew and Maria, make the transition after Mark, their long time property manager's death. Now laying there, afraid to wake the man holding her and the boys snoring in the room adjacent to hers; she lay staring at the ceiling as the sun's rays permeated through the thin curtains. As summer turned into fall, she knew that it was time to make another life altering decision.

Nicole, a registered nurse by degree, had spent the summer working at a hunting lodge deep in the woods in northern Maine. She had never intended to end up there but after experiencing the death of her husband earlier in the year, and the loss of several of her best friends that she had worked with; she had gone on an extended road trip with her beloved dog. Her odyssey had taken she and Neiko, her German shepherd, hiking and camping throughout the Adirondack Mountains of upstate New York, through the White Mountains of New Hampshire and eventually into Maine, where her destination had originally been Arcadia National Park. Fate had intervened and she never made it to the coast. After picking up a lone hitch hiker, who was battling his own demons, Nicole reluctantly offered him a ride to The Lodge, a hunting and fishing paradise for families and soldiers alike. The Lodge was a safe haven for injured members of the military who needed a solace from the realities of what they'd experienced while serving their country. Andrew, the owner of the Lodge for over forty years, was a proud member of the Wounded Warrior Program. He offered free room and board to any serviceman or woman who needed a respite, whether they came for a weekend or a week. It was because of this program that she and Aedan's paths crossed; that, and because she had nearly run him down with her truck while traveling in New Hampshire. While definitely getting off on the wrong foot, Nicole had not been impressed during their first encounter, but for some reason, her dog liked him and maybe that was the only reason, she'd given him a chance. Feeling only a little guilty about nearly clipping him with the trailer she had been towing at the time, she had vowed to only provide him with a ride to his destination. Now here she was, nearly five months later, still at the lodge and rediscovering love again, with the man that she had continuously dismissed.

She felt his shallow, steady breathing as he lay asleep beside her, and she silently thanked God for his tenacity, but mostly for his patience and understanding regarding her need to heal from the loss of her husband and friends, before she could offer him anything but her friendship.

Although no one would believe her, since her near brush with death, Aedan had slept beside her every night. But that was it, they slept together, but only to hold each other and comfort each other when the demons in their dreams returned. Aedan knew of the tragedies that Nicole had experienced and respected her enough to take the relationship that had recently turned the corner from tolerance to friendship, slow. After nearly losing her to a psychotic serial killer, he'd been forced to face the reality that somehow, sometime during the summer, he'd fallen in love with her, and that made him realize that he was never going to leave her side again, if he could help it. If their relationship continued down the path it was on, he knew that sooner or later he would have to tell her everything, including what those nine months living in the desert had cost him. Sure, she knew that he'd lost part of his leg, and had accepted his prosthetic without questions or comments. When she had inadvertently learned that he was not a handyman, as he had originally led her to think, but was in fact a doctor, she treated him the same, proving that his status was irrelevant. There was nothing superficial about Nicole Brentwood, he realized now. That fact alone made him love her even more.

As Aedan snored lightly beside her, she silently slipped out from under the quilted blankets of her bed, and quickly put on a robe. The crisp fall air reminded her that snow was just around the corner and she would have to move on soon as the Lodge would be closed up and winterized before long. But with her brother and soon to be sister-in-law currently inhabiting the home that she had shared with her deceased husband; Nicole didn't feel that it was hers anymore. She suddenly felt not only alone, but homeless. And with the addition of their beautiful daughter Lauren Rachel, she knew that the new parents needed more space than their tiny townhouse afforded. As she sat outside her cabin overlooking the river, Nicole decided then and there what she would do. She would never love another home the way she did the one on Oneida Lake, and 1990 Sycamore Lane would forever be in her heart. But that chapter of her life was over and every dream and aspiration that she had had during the time she'd spent there with Jared, died the day that the love of her life passed away in her arms after a senseless car accident.

She sat silently dividing her attention between the majestic hawk that flew above the roaring river in front of her, and her two beloved dogs that had joined her when she had exited the cabin. Jared had given her Neiko, a very energetic year old shepherd, when they had first moved into their new home.   Sinjin, her latest addition was a belated birthday present. While hiking one day, she and Aedan had found the half-starved, half dead pup trapped in a hunter's snare a few months ago and after rescuing him from certain death, had left him in the capable hands of the local vet.   Neither had expected him to pull through. Now here he was, part of her family for less than a month, and had already made his way into both she and Neiko's heart. She smiled to herself as she watched the dogs' romp and run, nip at each other and play tug-a-war with one stick after another. Her new four legged friend wasn't the only thing that had weaseled its' way into her heart. She would never forget the one and only love of her life, but maybe, just maybe, it was time to let the last layer of ice surrounding her heart, finally melt. She had spent all summer surrounded by people who had been virtual strangers to her just a few months ago and now, were some of the most important people in her life. Who knew what the future would hold for her, she thought to herself as she sat in the faded green Adirondack chair. But one thing was for certain; she would never forget the love and generosity that both Andrew and Maria had bestowed upon her. They had taken her in and accepted her without question, had given her a job and purpose. And they had not only supported her when questioned by the authorities, but had her back when a knife totting killer had set his sights on her. Both Andrew and Maria had been ready to protect her, die for her if necessary and Nicole knew that that kind of loyalty could never be forgotten. And then there was Aedan. What was she going to do with him? Or more importantly, what she was going to do without him, she thought now as she heard him silently open the door and join her. They had spent nearly every day of the last four months together and had become intertwined in each other's routines and lives and she would genuinely miss him when they went their separate ways in a week or so. Suddenly she felt panicked when she thought of the future. In his uncanny way, he sensed the second the panic set in. Instead of rushing to her, he simply sat down beside her and gently squeezed her hand. In his usual fashion, he didn't smother her or sugar-coat anything. He simply looked out at the rushing water in front of him and casually asked, "You're up early Nicki. Everything ok?" his voice conveyed what his facial expression did not.

"Yeah," she said as she continued to look forward, not making eye contact with the man beside her. "I was just watching the boys play and wondering where I go from here." She turned to square herself to him and searched his piercing light blue eyes for understanding. "Aedan, I can't go back. I don't think I can return to the hospital like nothing happened. I can't just walk onto that unit and work every day there like my friends didn't matter. Those women were not only my co-workers who were so savagely gunned down. They were some of my closest friends and while I realize that I am not the one who killed them, I still can't get past the fact that if I hadn't called a code manpower and had those two men thrown off my unit a few days before the attack happened, there wouldn't have been an attack and my best friends would still be alive." She fought the tears and continued. "I know that I have to return to nursing and I'm okay with that, because you see," she smiled, "I'm actually a pretty good nurse. Sure I ball break a lot and buck the system sometimes but all in all, I love being a nurse and before the shooting happened, I loved going to work every day. Now I just have to figure out where I can return to being a nurse. I just don't think I can return to Syracuse, I just don't think I can do it Aedan," she said as she appeared to slump in self-defeat.

"Then don't return to Syracuse Nic. Jimmy and Gwen are maintaining your home, and you still have what, three or four more months of extended leave from the hospital?" he continued, "So don't go back there yet. Why not try your hand at generic nursing first and see if you can handle it in a different setting and then if you can, you can weigh your options and go forward."

"You sound like you've been giving this some thought Aedan. What are you up to or what are you suggesting," she asked, slightly accusatorily.

"I'm not suggesting anything. But like you, it's time that I face my own fears and return to my chosen profession and serve people in the way that I was trained to do. After speaking with Danny last week, there is a job opportunity where I'm going, that might be of interest to you as well. She's stoned me almost nightly to discuss it with you but I never wanted to brooch the subject and make you feel like I'm pressuring you into doing anything you can't or don't want to do."

"Interesting," she thought to herself. "Okay, so you and your sister have some job opportunity that you think I might be interested in. I'm already sitting, so why don't you just lay it on me and tell me about it," she chuckled when seeing his almost nervous expression.

"Okay," he stammered, never taking his eyes off of her. "My sister lives in northern New Hampshire in a little tight knit community on the border of Maine and basically a stone's throw from Canada. Seems that they lost the only physician in town and the clinic can't operate without one. Danielle was approached by the mayor asking if I would be interested in filling in, even if only on a temporary basis until they can find someone full time. I don't honestly know what the pay is, nor do I really care. I just sort of believe that everything happens for a reason Nicki, and I think that their doctor leaving on a whim a few weeks ago was fate and it's possibly my destiny to take his place, you know, sort of ease me back into medicine."

"Okay, and that might be Aedan. What has that got to do with me?" she asked, more intrigued than actually interested.

"Well, it seems that when their doc left, he took the only RN on the staff with him," he laughed. Those folks have had no one to look after them for their various aches and pain, headaches and sprains since he skipped out of town and anyone who needs attention has been forced to drive almost an hour to the nearest urgent care or hospital. No, it's not what I aspire to do for the rest of my life, but the way I see it, it could be something to get me back practicing medicine and tide me over the winter until I know what I want to do with the rest of my life, and will help their community out as well. So, what do you say Nic? Will you at least consider the possibility of helping me run the clinic?" he asked with a twinkle in his eye and an innocent smile so sincere that it made his dimples come out more. She looked at the man sitting three feet from her and although he looked absolutely nothing like her deceased husband, she couldn't help but think of Jared and the way he would give her that same conniving look when he wanted something but already knew how she'd answer. God she missed him so much and not a day passed that he didn't enter her mind. There was always something that reminded her of his gentle nature and the hawk soaring overhead this cool morning was yet another reminder of what she'd lost.   Now looking at the soldier/surgeon/blue-eyed man staring back at her waiting for her to respond to his proposition; she began to realize that fate had caused to her lose one great man in her life, but it also allowed her to meet another.

"Sounds like you've thought this out thoroughly during the last week or so. You're just springing this on me now and I really think I'll need to take some time to give your proposition some thought," she said, less than enthusiastically. Seeing the frown subconsciously coming across his face, she quickly responded spontaneously, "okay, I've thought about it and yes." He looked at her in shock. "Yes?"

"Yes Aedan. Yes, I'll help you run the clinic. Yes, I'll work with you, but not for you," she said savoring his smile. "We'll be a team, and you will NOT be my boss. Deal?" she said, smiling back at him.

"You'll do it Nicki? You'll come with me to New Hampshire to run the clinic? Oh my God, I love you," he exclaimed not thinking about what he was saying. He jumped to his feet, pulled her out of her chair and took her into his arms, twirling her around with him. Neiko and Sinjin came running to her side hearing her squealing and laughing as they spun round and round holding on to one another, finally collapsing into each other's arms onto the grass below. Neiko was the first to start licking Aedan's face, followed by the still skittish pup, who came to Nicole's side. She pushed herself up onto her elbow and started drilling him with questions.

"Where will we live? How many people do you think they see a day? I don't know Aedan, I've never worked outside of a hospital setting before. The thought kind of scares me. Does Danielle have room for us and the dogs? I'm not going if we can't bring the dogs Aedan, you know that right?" she continued drilling him with questions. He continued to grin as he let her ramble on. "When will we go to New Hampshire? Are they expecting you right away? Sounds like they need you sooner, rather than later. Have you told Andrew and Maria yet? Oh my, we can't just leave them high and dry Aedan, we can't."

"There you go again love, talking for an entire minute straight without taking one breath. You are something else Nicole Brentwood, and I can't wait to tell Danielle

11

and Bruce that you'll be joining me on this adventure. In the short time that she spent with you, Danny came to really care about you Nicki, and she'll be thrilled that you're coming with me. And regarding where to stay, if you're okay with it, she already has a place lined up for us and the dogs. That is, if you're okay continuing to share living accommodations with me."

"Why wouldn't I be? We've spent the last few months sharing a cabin. Why would it be any different there?" she asked tentatively, already knowing that any other setting than the lodge would change the dynamics for both of them.

"Well," he spoke hesitantly, "When I told Danny that I'd come fill in, at least temporarily for their MIA doc, I told her that I would only do it under one condition. The deal breaker was, I insisted that I have my own place, so she found me one. Bruce found me, us, a tiny log cabin that we can live in very affordably. It's located just outside of town but from the pictures she's sent me and the description, it's pretty isolated, located at the end of a dead end dirt road and sets on 30 acres and is nestled alongside a river, with a huge mountain range adjacent. It reminded me of here so I said yes, sight unseen. I thought that if I saw the river every day, it would remind me of you."

"You picked out a place to stay because you didn't want to forget me Aedan?" she asked, feeling the last patch of ice finally melting away from her heart.

"Nicki, whether you came or not, whether there is a river or not, I could never forget you nor would I want to. Haven't you figured it out by now, you hold my heart Nicole. Somewhere along the line, I fell in love with you. That simple, I love you lady, and I'm so very glad that you're joining me on this next adventure. But there is a catch. The log cabin only has one bedroom;

hope that's not going to be a problem."

She squeezed the hand still holding hers and smiled. "I don't think it's going to be a problem at all."

Chapter 2

They spent the next week helping Andrew and Maria winterize and close down The Lodge. Nicole hadn't realized just how much work went into shutting down a camp as large as Andrew's. She and Aedan worked alongside the owners and the remaining staff, and Nicole couldn't help but find it bittersweet to be closing yet another chapter of her life.

"You know," Maria said quietly as they continued to pack, "I expect you and Aedan to come visit us again next summer Nicole, and I'll be thoroughly pissed off if you don't make it back here for at least a week or two. And if things don't work out at the clinic or with Aedan for that matter, I hope you know that you are always welcome to stay with us, whether it's here at the lodge or at our winter home in Hyannis. You're family now Nicki, and don't you ever forget that!" she said, wiping a lone tear from her eye.

"I know Maria and I promise you, I will come back to visit next summer. You couldn't keep me away from here. I can't think of any other place that could possibly offer me serenity and peace like this place does. And I'd love to bring my momma and father up here next year if that's okay with you and Andrew. They'd love it here. If you think I can cook, wait until you try my momma's recipes, she's absolutely amazing!"

"I'm sure she is amazing. How couldn't she be after raising such an incredible daughter," she said as she stood, hugging the younger woman beside her.

"I'm going to miss you and Aedan so much and I just know that things are going to work for you two. Maybe this time next year Danny won't be the only one trying for a baby" Maria whispered into her ear.

Pulling away, Nicole looked shocked before responding. "Maria is," she didn't finish the sentence before Maria answered. "Oh no, Danielle's not pregnant yet. But she longs for a baby, just the way you will someday Nicole. You don't know it yet, but the circle will be complete for you someday, and Aedan will help you complete it."

"No Maria. I had everything the way it was supposed to be when I was married to Jared. My opportunity passed and we don't get second chances. Part of me loves Aedan, I really do. But it'll never be the same as it was with Jared and I'll never get married again," she said, trying to convince the matriarch of the lodge, and herself.

"You're right. It'll never be the same as it was with your first husband Nicole. It's not supposed to be, for that was a different time and he was a different man than the one you love now. But even though it's different, love is love and it's your destiny to be loved again. Through that love, you'll make beautiful babies together; and be blessed with a long happy life together."

Nicole allowed the words to absorb and simply shook her head as the tears started to flow.

"I would love to believe you Maria and I'd love to think that I'll be completely and profoundly in love again and have children someday but unfortunately, I don't think that's in the cards for me anymore. I'm thirty years old and neither Aedan nor I are in any position to think that far into the future. And by the time I'm ready to make that kind of commitment, if I'm ever ready again, it'll be far too late and I'll be far too old to think about bringing a child into this world, let alone children. And while I appreciate your wisdom and insight, and yes I know you have an uncanny sixth sense, this is one time you're wrong. I am destined to remain alone in this life. But it's okay, I've accepted it and my world is complete as long as I have friends like you in it. I love you both so much Maria and I hope you realize that I couldn't have made it through the summer without your friendship, understanding and love."

"Oh honey," she sniffled, wiping more tears from her eyes. You will be happy again. I swear to you, you'll be so happy again and are already so loved and you'll realize that in time, as well" Maria said, looking at the beautiful woman standing beside her. "Promise me one thing as you leave here Nicole. Promise me that you'll give Aedan and love a chance; he needs it as much as you do."

"Aedan's my best friend Maria, well that is along with Gwen. I wish nothing but the best for him, I really do."

"I know Nicole, I know," Maria responded, smiling. "And he already has the best because he's in love with you," she thought to herself.

Chapter 3

As the week wound down, Nicole packed up her belongings after she and Aedan had assisted Maria and Andrew in closing the vacant guest cabins and most of the lodge. Suddenly she realized just how much she was going to miss her surrogate parents. She had spent more time with the two owners of the Lodge than she had with her own parents since her youth. And as of tomorrow, it would be just she and Aedan, and her two dogs of course, traveling alone to another state to start another life. The thought was beginning to terrify her. Sure, she had spent some quality time with Aedan's twin sister Danielle and her now fiancée Bruce, but Aedan had been right when he asked if she was going to be okay living in a one bedroom cabin with him. The entire dynamics of their friendship were about to change and that idea was a little unsettling. Yes, he made her laugh, and made her cry, placated her and inspired her, reassured her and frequently irritated the hell out of her. But at the end of it all, he made her smile and forced her to enjoy life again. But now, they were actually starting another chapter of their lives, and in essence, moving in together. Even though she had fantasized about him from time to time, and couldn't help but acknowledge that he had an incredibly muscular body, she had never really considered being intimate with him. She loved sex as much as the next person. The vibes that Aedan emitted were enough to ascertain that he'd be more than willing to help her out in that department, and probably do a very fine job of it. But being the gentleman that he was, he'd never tried to get her into bed. Now, they were moving into a cozy tiny cabin in the middle of nowhere with no lodge owners nor guests interrupting their day to day routine and schedule. Nicole realized that one way or another, she would have to address their relationship, even though it was still in its' infancy.

"Maybe I should just sleep with him tonight and get it over with," she thought to herself as she continued to pack with her dogs sleeping just feet away.

Aedan entered the cabin to hear her humming in the back room. He enjoyed moments like this, when she was relaxed and thinking that she was alone, she'd let her guard down and was truly stress-free. Her voice, as evidenced by the several times over the summer they'd serenaded the various guests who had made their way to The Lodge for a weekend fishing trip or a week long hiatus from reality, was angelic and soft, yet resonated her inner strength when she sang alone, thinking no one was within earshot. She played a mean classical guitar and with he, Maria and Andrew accompanying her on their respective instruments, they'd put on a great show for their guests on more than one occasion. He was going to miss those evenings and silently hoped that with the move to New

Hampshire, he would have an opportunity to get to know the woman behind the sad green eyes even more.

Not wanting to startle her, he coughed just loud enough to get her shepherd's attention. Neiko immediately rose and bound towards him, with Sinjin, their newly acquired pup at his feet. Even after nearly having his paw severed in a hunter's snare, the young dog raced to keep up with Neiko. Seeing their movement, Nicole who had been lost in thought, stopped humming and looked up and into the piercing light blue eyes of the man who'd come to mean more to her than she was willing to admit.

"Oh hey Aedan," she smiled. Embarrassed at what she had just been thinking about him, she felt herself blush and was silently thankful that he couldn't read her mind.

"Oh hey yourself gorgeous," he responded back, smiling. "I see you've got your helpers in here supervising your packing" he joked, as he crouched down to be eye level with the two dogs and their wagging tails.

"Yup, they were so much help," she laughed.

"I've loaded everything that I can into the bed of your truck Nicki. Is there anything you want me to carry out for you? I was thinking that we should get an early start tomorrow so we can get to Danny's and the new place while we still have most of the day to get settled. They'll want us to open up the clinic first thing Monday morning. So if we can get settled into the cabin between tomorrow and Friday, that'll leave us Saturday and Sunday to get groceries for the cabin and organize the clinic. I don't know about you," he added when he saw an apprehensive look starting to come over her face, "but I'm getting a little nervous about being in charge of this clinic. I certainly hope that the two care attendants and the office manager/secretary can direct us onto the right track to get the place up and running smoothly. This is all new to me and I'm used to just walking into organized chaos, not being in charge of everything."

"This whole clinic thing is new to me as well Aedan and I'm getting a little spooked. I've always worked in a hospital setting and have always had other staff around for back up in an emergency. It's kind of scary thinking that there's only me and you."

"I'm sure you're a great nurse Nicki. I can promise you, I will always have your back."

She knew that the final layer around her heart had completely melted when she saw the sincerity in his eyes. She knew at that very moment that it was possible to love twice in one life. And she knew that she would never do anything to hurt him intentionally.

"I am a great nurse Aedan, and I know that we'll make a kick ass team! So let's finish packing the last things that we can tonight and enjoy the evening with Andrew and Maria. I'm going to miss this place Aedan. I promised Maria that I'd come back, we'd come back, next summer if things work out."

"We'll be back," was all he said. With those three words, she knew that their relationship had moved beyond simply friendship.

Chapter 4

Andrew and Aedan, along with the last few members of Andrew's staff marveled at the gourmet meal spread out in front of them when they entered the dining room. How had Nicole and Maria managed such a feast they all wondered, when basically the entire lodge had already been packed up and loaded for their departure in the morning. Nicole and Maria saluted each other with their respective wine glasses as they watched the men's eyes dart from one corner of the table to the other, with all of them salivating.

"Think I'd like to kiss the cook," Andrew exclaimed, drawing his long time love into his arms and kissing her squarely on the lips.

"You kiss me like that again love," she chuckled, "And you're gonna miss dinner."

He winked at her lovingly, "Ah but honey, I think I'd enjoy the dessert!" he teased back.

Aedan laughed as he saw Nicole blush at the older couple's blatant display of affection as they appeared oblivious of their guests. "Hey you two, get a room. The rest of us want to dig in, if that's alright with you."

Still held tight in Andrew's embrace, Maria burst out chuckling.

"Suit yourself Aedan, dig in. But I would prefer my man's loving and dessert over this thrown together meal any day of the week. And if our Nicole doesn't make you think along those same lines, then you two are definitely doing something wrong."

Both Nicole and Aedan reacted and responded simultaneously, nearly drowning out each other. Neither could be understood as they tried to assure everyone that romance was not part of their agenda and that they were just friends. The more they both carried on adamantly about the fact that they were just friends, the more Maria and Andrew both were convinced that the two of them truly were hooked on one another. Though Andrew wanted to let them go on and on as he found it humorous, Maria interrupted them so as to not let their dinner go cold.

"Alright, alright. We know, you're just friends. We've got it, so now let's eat before the whole meal is cold and ruined," Maria intervened, motioning for everyone to take a seat.

They spent the next hour laughing and devouring an amazing feast as everyone exchanged tales and stories from the summer. A few jabs were directed at the lodge owner, who gave more than his far share back to the men and women around him, all of whom he considered family. At the end of the meal, all helped clear the table in relative silence as they knew that it was the end to yet another wonderful summer spent in the middle of nowhere in the mountains of Maine.

In the beginning, when Aedan had convinced Nicole to simply give him a ride into the lodge. There was no possible way that Nicole would have ever imagined that this remote setting would be a place that she would come to love and never want to leave. But when she finally got to see a moose, a lifelong dream of hers, on her way into the lodge, and then she saw the Lodge itself, she was captivated just like everyone else who made the arduous journey into the woods. Over the course of the summer, she had earned her keep working as their cook, and somewhere along the way, she had started to enjoy life again. Her life was vastly different than the one she had lived just one year prior. Now a widow, with no place to call home, and no longer employed at the hospital where she had started her career after graduating nursing school; she was at yet another crossroads in life. Sensing the silent emotional turmoil swirling in her head, Maria waited until they were alone in the kitchen before she turned to face the young woman whom she had come to love like her own daughter.

"Are you excited about running the clinic Nicki," she said innocently. "Because Aedan might have the initials of MD after his name but we both know who's going to be in charge, now don't we girl?" she chuckled.

Turning to face the older woman who'd become her surrogate mother, she revealed the tears that she'd been trying so hard to hide. Seeing her angst, Maria went to her side and hugged her warmly.

"Dry those eyes Nicole, and dry them right now baby girl. There'll be no sadness here tonight, you hear me? This is a new beginning for you, and not all of us get second chances. So you wipe those tears, chin up, and promise me that you're going to drive to Errol tomorrow and then to Danielle's and open that clinic with Aedan and give those folks what they've been without for far too long. You and our Aedan are going to have the clinic up and running in no time and the people of that community need you and I don't expect you to let them down, you hear me," she announced sternly, knowing that Nicole was floundering in her ability to try nursing again.

"What if I can't do it Maria? What if I can't be a nurse anymore? The last time I was one, seven of my co-workers and best friends died because of me," she whispered.

"Oh Bull shit!" the elder woman snapped.

"Your co-workers did NOT die because of you! They were killed in cold blood by two crazed men, two murderers who would have unleashed their carnage whether it had been you or one of the other nurses who'd had them removed from the unit. You are NOT to blame for someone else's actions and I don't want to ever hear you take accountability for what they did again. Just like you're not to blame for your husband's car accident, you are not to blame for your friends' deaths. End of discussion. Now," she said calmly as she released her embrace and sauntered over to the pantry, removing the last remaining item on the shelf.

"Let's go join the men and wrap this season up in style!"

They laughed, cried, sang and drank half the night away as they sat around the last bonfire of the summer season. The seven of them sang along with Nicole as she played her guitar until her fingers were too numb to feel the strings. As they huddled under blankets, comforters and anything that would keep the encroaching winter's bite at bay, Nicole realized that she'd been wrong earlier in the evening. She did have a home. Here in the mountains of northern Maine, down a 16-mile stretch of dirt road nestled between a river with its huge rapids and swift current, and a majestic mountain range as its backdrop, was her home. Andrew and Maria might not be blood related to her, but they were about as close to family as anyone could ever wish for. In that moment, she realized that she was home after all.

Chapter 5

Whether it was the amount of Winter Jack she'd consumed the night before, the crisp temperature in the cabin despite the wood stove, or sheer exhaustion; Nicole woke much later than usual the following morning and couldn't believe that Aedan had let her stay in bed until nearly 7am, despite the fact that they had a big day ahead of them. She quickly dressed and was caught by an amazing aroma emitting from the kitchen the second she opened her bedroom door. She scanned the tiny cabin in search of her dogs and laughed when she saw the two of them sitting patiently at Aedan's feet as he stood with his back to her, and was concentrating on whatever he had cooking on the stove top. She wasn't sure what it was, but sweet Jesus it smelled good! Trying to not startle the three men in her life, she cleared her throat gently. When he slowly turned around and smiled, her heart instantly warmed. Yup, she'd done it, she thought to herself as she crouched down to greet her two dogs bounding towards her. She'd fallen for the soft spoken ex-soldier, hook, line and sinker.

"Good Morning, whatcha making," she asked, looking up and smiling.

Momentarily silent, thinking in his mind that even half awake, with her mussed up hair, bathrobe on cock-eyed and morning breath, Nicole still was one of the most beautiful, wholesome and genuine women he'd ever met. He knew that one of the things that made her so attractive, in his mind's eye, was that she was not vain, like his ex-fiancée.   She wasn't superficial and materialistic like some of the other women he'd dated over the years who once they found out he was a doctor. In the past, many women had just assumed that he was loaded and would spend vast amounts of money on elaborate frivolous gifts just because he had the initials MD after his name. He'd seen Nicole both dressed up and fancy, and dressed down and casual, and had known from the beginning that she was genuine.   What you saw was what you got when it came to Nicole Rose Brentwood. His mind went back to his first exposure to her, when they'd first met on the summit of St. Regis Mountain, in the northern Adirondacks months ago and he'd looked into her sad eyes and was gone, just like that. Of course, back then, she'd completely blown him off and walked out of his life as quickly as she'd entered it. Thank God for fate; that, and the fact that she'd nearly killed him while towing her dilapidated camper on a country road in New Hampshire. If he hadn't been hitchhiking at the moment she'd rounded the bend just a little too fast and nearly clipped him with her jackknifing camper, their paths might never have crossed again. Yes, he thought as he smiled back at her, as he walked toward her, offering his hand to help her up, thank God for fate and second chances.

"Good morning gorgeous," he said as he helped her stand. Pulling a little too hard, the momentum nearly launched her into his arms, but she didn't resist. Looking up into his crystal blue eyes, she laughed at their close proximity.

"Well good morning to you too handsome. It smells wonderful in here Aedan, but you didn't have to go to such trouble," she said almost nervously. "We have a big day ahead of us so I didn't think you'd have time for such a fancy meal."

Still holding her close, he whispered, "There's always time to do something that feels right," and with that, he pulled her closer and kissed her. He kissed her like she'd never been kissed before, like a man drowning and she was his lifeline. When they finally separated, she laughed, putting her hands on his chest and gently pushing, "Hey, sunshine, get your ass back to that stove and cook me my meal! I'm going to take a quick shower if that's ok with you and pack the last of my stuff in the truck."

"Take your time Nic, I've got this covered."

"Thanks Aedan. Come on boys, let's leave him alone so he can cook us a feast," she said, patting her leg, calling her dogs as she turned and walked toward the bathroom. She heard Aedan murmur "Traitors" as the dogs quickly followed her in.

Chapter 6

After finishing up their last meal of the season in their little cabin, and helping Andrew winterize it, the time had come to finally say good bye to the owners of the lodge. Leaving what had been home to both of them for the last several months was bittersweet. Nicole packed the last of their belongings into her truck and now it was time to do what she had been dreading for the last few days. The four of them stood together in the yard with the two pups running around their legs, chasing each other and the ball that Aedan tossed to focus on something other than saying farewell to two of the most important people in his life. Sure, he was leaving Andrew and Maria to move to his sister's town so he would have family close by; but in his mind's eye, the owners of the Lodge were just as much family to him as his own twin sister was. It was Maria that finally gave them the shove to finally get them going.

"Hey you two, not that we don't like you or anything, but times a wasting and you have a long drive ahead of you to get to Danielle's and your new home so as much as we love you, get the hell out of here," she laughed. Walking up to Aedan, she took him into her arms and held him tight before planting a gentle kiss on his cheek. "You make sure you take care of our girl Aedan. Or I'll hunt you down myself. Love you, you know," she whispered in his ear.

And pulling away, she added, loud enough to everyone to hear, "I expect you to bring our Nicole back to us next summer, ya hear?"

"Yes mam! I promise you Maria, we'll be back. And I love you too, love you like the momma I lost so long ago." With a tear in his eye, he smiled at the matriarch of the Lodge, "We'll be back. You have my word."

Seeing the exchange warmed his heart. Andrew too, said his good byes by taking the ex-soldier, AKA their handyman into a huge bear hug similar to the one Maria gave him, sans the kiss.

"You need anything son when you're setting up that clinic, you call and we'll be there. Anything at all, that simple. Now get on out of here before you get my woman blatting."

Aedan nodded in understanding and called the dogs to load them into the back seat so Nicole could say her good-byes without distractions. Andrew was first to approach her. Seeing the tears already welling up into her eyes, he grabbed her and held her tight.

"We love you baby girl and this is not the end of our friendship. If this clinic gig doesn't work out, you know you have a home here with us next spring and don't you ever forget it. You and Aedan are going to be such an asset to that little town; but if at any time he's driving you crazy and you need a break, you just get into that truck of yours and come visit us on the cape okay? You are always welcome whether it's here or there, and we are always just a call away."

Andrew turned so that he could wipe the tears from his eyes.

Maria watched the exchange between her long time love and the woman who was, as far as she was concerned, a second daughter. Always having a strong sixth sense, partly thanks to her Native American heritage, Maria knew that Nicole was going to love her new home and next chapter in her life, but that was something that Nicole had to learn and discover on her own. Knowing that she would never be alone again brought Maria comfort as she looked into the deep green eyes of the woman who'd become her best friend. Words didn't need to be exchanged as the women looked at one another before embracing one last time. "There are so many things that I could say to you right now baby girl but I only have one thing I want you to take with away with you," she said quietly. "One of the hardest things in life is letting go Nicole. Whether you're letting go of guilt, anger, loss or love; change is never easy. Always remember we fight to hold on and we fight to let go. I know that you'll never forget the love you shared with Jared, and no one expects you to; but when you travel down the road today and leave us, leave the anger, guilt and pain here as you start your new life in New Hampshire okay? Go into this next chapter with a clean mind and unburdened soul; promise me mi amor."

"Oh Maria," she said as tears flowed freely down her face. "I could never, nor would I want to, forget Jared. He was my first love and the most important person in my life for nearly a decade. He will always be with me and in my heart; but this summer has taught me that my heart is large enough to love two people. And yes, I love Aedan. While it's different from what I had with Jared, it's still love and I feel blessed to have him and you both" looking at both she and Andrew, "in my life. We will be back to visit you next summer, promise" she said as she held on tight to the woman whom she loved as much as her own mother. Knowing that final good byes were hard and watching the exchange between them tug on his own heart, Aedan gently tapped on the horn of the truck and shouted "Hey, come on woman, are we going to get out of here sometime before dark" he jested. "Let's move it honey or Neiko, Sinjin and I are going to haul ass and leave you behind," he laughed. Nicole flipped him off as she held Maria's hand for a few more seconds, feeling the elder woman's strength and energy flow into her. Squeezing it tightly before letting go, Nicole smiled and simply said, "Until someday…" And with that, Nicole turned and walked towards Aedan and what lay ahead for them in New Hampshire.

Chapter 7

They traveled down the dirt road in relative silence for the first several miles, both lost in their own thoughts. While Aedan was hypothetically reviewing in his head what types of patients he should expect to walk through the doors of the clinic, Nicole was wondering how they were going to adjust to their new living arrangements. Finally breaking the silence, she turned toward him as he navigated the logging road carefully, trying to avoid potholes large enough to envelope a tire if run over.

"Aedan, you said that the cabin we're going to be staying in is off the grid correct? I really don't know a thing about solar power or electricity powered by windmills so I really hope that there's someone to show us the ropes on how we store the energy or what we need to do to keep everything operational. I mean, is it something that just keeps producing energy now that the systems are in place or do we have to do something with them to make the energy work? How many appliances can be working at once and what if there's no sun, or no wind; what then? I love the idea, really I do. But I don't know a thing about that kind of alternative energy, do you?"

Hearing her, he just burst out laughing.

"There you go again love, asking four or five questions all in one breath. I have never understood how you do that without getting hypoxic."

She laughed too, knowing that he was right.

"Hey, don't you make fun of me! I can't help it I have good lung capacity!"

"Oh Nicole, that you do. Regarding your questions, since we decided to live in an off the grid home, I've been doing a little research on them since I too have had minimal experience with them. One good thing about it is that more than half the people living in the area where we're heading utilize some form of alternative energy, including Danielle and Bruce, so we'll have plenty of resources when we've got questions or need help. The cabin also has a much larger wood stove than we had at Drew's, and I don't think the cabin will be all that much bigger than his, so I'm guessing that alone, will provide us with our main heat source. Bruce already offered to stock it up during the day when we're at the clinic. That is as long as your two killer dogs will let him through the door," he chuckled.

"Neiko knows him, and even though it'll be a new environment, he'll let him in. And the pup's still too timid to chase anyone off so I wouldn't expect him to have any difficulties entering. Now if a stranger entered, whether I'm there or not, different story all together," she added.

"I know," Aedan said, thinking back to what Neiko had done to Mark, the man who had held her captive. He'd never seen such brutality to a man's neck, even during his stent in the desert. Neiko had dove through a window to rescue his master, and literally obliterated the man holding her captive. When the dog was finally called off, there was nothing distinguishable left of his neck or throat. And for that, Aedan would be forever in debt to man's best friend. Now here they were, bounding down the dirt road with the dogs curled up in the back sleep snoozing without a care in the world. And he couldn't be happier.

Chapter 8

Even though they weren't towing her antique camping trailer on the way out from camp, Nicole was secretly thankful that Aedan had offered to drive the winding dirt road and over the bridge covering the Raging River. The bridge had been recently replaced and was no longer a single lane wooden covered bridge like the one that had terrified Nicole earlier in the summer when she first encountered it.

Now it was steel and two lanes wide, but still seemed to sway like the racing current just a few feet below. Teasing her, Aedan stopped half way across the wide expanse of the river. Turning to him with a slightly panicked look, Nicole wondered what was wrong and why he was stopping.

"Relax Nicole. This bridge would hold an 18 wheeler so I think it can handle your truck. I just thought you'd like to stop to take a few pictures of the river before we left."

"Are you crazy Aedan, you know I hate heights and you can't just stop in the middle of the road! What if someone comes flying around the corner and hits us head on!"

"Okay," he said as he slowly put the truck back into gear. "Sorry Bullwinkle, she doesn't want to take your picture today," was all he needed to say to get her full attention.

"What? Stop the truck," she nearly screamed! "Bullwinkle, as in moose? There's a moose down there Aedan," she shouted, grabbing her camera and leaping out of the vehicle before it had come to a complete halt. Not seeing it immediately, she turned to Aedan with an accusatory look.

"Where? And so help me God, you'd better not be bull shitting me about the moose Aedan!"

"I'm not. Stop talking and look over your right shoulder Nicki." She did as he said and gasped. There, less than 100 yards upstream was a huge bull moose. Having already shed his antlers, Nicole wasn't sure its' sex at first, but to her, it didn't matter. The moose stood chest deep in water, oblivious to the near frigid temperature as it moved its' massive head from side to side, as if looking for fish. Nicole got off several shots before the moose abruptly ended her impromptu photo session. Aedan waited in the truck with the two shepherds, bribing them with treats to keep them quiet, while Nicole took one last look at the magnificent creature as it walked away from them and into the woods. When she finally got back into her truck, she was momentarily speechless, still in awe that not only had they seen a moose on the way in to the Lodge, but also on the way out. The same river flowed directly in front of the main lodge and its' many cabins, yet never once did Nicole see a moose during their entire summer residing there. Whether it was this particular area that they frequented or Aedan just had an eye for spotting them, she didn't care, she was just ecstatic to have her first and last sightings of such a magnificent animal in the company of Aedan and her beloved dogs. She was certain that this would be a memory that she'd cherish forever.

Looking at her traveling companion, she smiled. "Guess I owe you another. Thank You Aedan," she said softly. She leaned over the seat of her truck and kissed him gently on the cheek.

"Thank you for having such amazing peripheral vision."

"If my peripheral vision were amazing Nic, I'd still have my leg. I didn't pay close enough attention once to my surroundings and you see what it cost me. It won't ever happen again."

"Does it still hurt you Aedan? Do you get that phantom pain that I've heard people talk about," she asked gently. Knowing she wasn't being nosy, just asking; he didn't hesitate talking to her about it.

"Didn't at first. Initially I had no pain, absolutely felt nothing. One minute you know I'm standing there, bull shitting with the guys and the next, I'm flying through the air, then darkness. Woke up in a helicopter being medivacked out because they knew I was going to lose the leg and I guess at that point they thought I wasn't even going to make the trip across the dessert. They kept me pretty out of it, compliments of Morphine so I can't honestly say I remember much. Next thing I know, it's 48 hours later and I'm in a hospital bed in Germany with the sheet hanging funny where my leg used to be. Then I knew something was very wrong; got word that I made out much better than two of my closest friends, and that hurt worse than the pain in what was left of my leg. Not sure what kind of nurse you are Nicole, but let me tell you, military nurses can be brutal. They gave me no slack, minimal sympathy, and told me point blank that I lost part of a leg, deal with it, and here's how to adjust to my new life. They didn't sugar coat how bad it would suck during the healing process, getting used to a prosthesis, and using crutches. God I hated those fucking things. So as soon as my leg healed, I pushed the right buttons until I could get fitted for a prosthetic."

She listened without comment or judgment, she just listened and tried to envision what those days, and weeks must have been like to just be doing his job and then having life as you know it, yanked out from underneath his feet and in a matter of seconds, losing everything important to him. And then it dawned on her. She'd had the same thing happen to her, and maybe that was why the connection she felt to Aedan was so strong. One minute she'd been a nurse simply caring for her patients, and the next she'd become a widow and had lost several of her best friends and co-workers to senseless violence, much the same way Aedan had lost his friends. Different circumstances, but the outcome was still the same. They'd both suffered unspeakable loss and both felt guilty that they'd lived when their friends had perished. Acting on impulse, and before she'd thought it through, she took a deep breath and simply said, "Aedan, could you please pull over for just a second?"

"Yeah, sure. You need to pee or what?" he asked, somewhat confused.

Laughing, she responded, "You're so eloquent with your vocabulary there sometimes soldier. Just pull over and throw it in park. Slightly perplexed, he did as she asked. Then turned and looked into her green eyes which seemed to glisten in the bright morning sunshine. He'd always thought that she had the most amazing green eyes, not hazel nor deep green. They took on the color of the ocean, and sometimes were the color of the many rolling green meadows he'd seen in Ireland, all in one. But at the moment, for whatever reason, they were very vaso-dilated and grey. He'd only seen them change to grey when she'd been thoroughly pissed at him, and very quickly tried to figure out what she could possibly be mad about. Before he had time to really evaluate the situation, she flipped up the armrest dividing their seats, and in one swift move, not only slid over towards him, but did a 180 so that she was now facing him and practically in his lap. She looked up into his piercing blue eyes and said nothing. Keeping eye contact with him, she leaned into him and brought her mouth up to his. Then everything exploded. That one move set in motion what had been coming on for weeks now, and neither cared about the future; they both just needed and savored the moment. Nicole commanded her dogs to stay, and then she and Aedan started ripping clothes off each other as if they needed to remove them in order to breathe. More than once, Aedan suggested that they throw a blanket down outside the truck, but Nicole didn't want to break the spell that they were both under and insisted that they stay right where they were. Watching her remove the last of her clothing, his approval of her body was very evident. Neither spoke, they just took. Foreplay was forgotten as they continued to kiss as Nicole climbed into his lap and rode him like her life depended on it. Oblivious to the steering wheel that was rubbing her back raw as she thrust up and down; she controlled the speed in the beginning but quickly got caught up in the pure ecstasy of being loved again, and before either realized it, their pace had increased to near panic level. And together they went over the edge.

Chapter 9

They dressed in silence, both lost in their own thoughts. Once the dogs were done watering all the trees in the vicinity and back into the truck, Aedan turned once again to Nicole, smiled and asked "Guess it's probably a little too late to ask if we should have used precautions?"

"Don't worry about it soldier, I've got you covered in that department. Oh, and Aedan," she slid him a sly smile, "I really enjoyed that. But since I'm going to probably need Silvadene for the rub burn on my back, think we could have round two in a real bed tonight?"

He only heard "round two," and "tonight", and responded according. "Anything you say Nic," and proceeded to throw the truck into drive, smiling, and started down the dirt road towards their new life.

Chapter 10

After their initial stop, they made good time heading down the logging trail, and back onto the main trail and towards New Hampshire. Once they had cell coverage, Aedan touched base with his sister, who, by the enthusiasm conveyed in her voice when she was on speakerphone, couldn't wait for them to arrive. She told them that she'd been up to the cabin with Bruce, and had it ready for the two of them when they arrived. Danielle went on to elaborate that she'd broken several fingernails and rubbed her knuckles raw cleaning the tiny cabin so that it'd be spotless. She described in great detail what their new home would be like and how she'd stocked the pantry with many of his favorite foods. Nicole interjected occasionally but for the most part, simply listened to the conversation between brother and sister. She found it comical that they were more than siblings, and as twins, they shared a stronger bond. If she were to bet, she doubted that they even realized that their brains were in sync with one another and that they subconsciously finished each other's sentences. She listened not so much to the words that they spoke, but the inflection in their voices and in their tones. She knew how much they loved one another, and she welcomed the opportunity to get to know his twin sister even better.

Remembering back to the first time she'd met Danielle atop St. Regis Mountain, near Paul Smith's College and immediately assumed, incorrectly, that the voluptuous blonde was Aedan's girlfriend, made her laugh to herself now. She'd been so jealous that someone could look as perfect as Danielle had after completing a challenging hike.

After the call was over, Nicole turned the radio on and chuckled as Aedan started humming to the Zac Brown song emitting from the speakers.

"Yes, life was good," was all she could think of as they bounced along the country road leading to the highway. Life was definitely starting to look promising again and for the first time in a long time, she looked forward to what the future had in store for her.

By the time they crossed the state line into New Hampshire, both were singing along to Janis Joplin, one of Nicole's favorite CD's as the dogs ignored them and slept soundly in the back seat. It was just after lunch when they hit the town limits and drove the remaining miles to Danny's; but not before driving by what was going to be their new job site. The massive white Victorian with its' wrap around porch looked like something out of Architectural Digest Nicole thought as they slowed the truck and gawked at the size of the building and its' ornate detailing.

"Looks really nice but it needs rocking chairs all across that huge porch don't you think?"

"Anything you want love."

She reached over, and gently rubbed her hand up the inside of his jeans.

"That's quite an opened ended statement; anything I want. I'll get back to you on that," she purred. Not quite sure what had gotten into her during the ride out from the lodge, but silently thanking God for whatever had awoken her libido, he just continued humming, trying to contain a certain part of his anatomy as it too was definitely intrigued by Nicole's change in demeanor.

After viewing the exterior of the clinic where they'd be caring for patients, Aedan pulled out his phone to plug in the address of their new home. Both took note of the towns' layout and where the grocery store, gas station, post office etcetera were as they slowly drove through the small New England town and toward the outskirts where their log cabin was situated. Just before reaching their destination, Aedan pointed down a winding dirt road.

"We'll head over there later once we get settled a bit. That's where Bruce and Danny live. You can't miss it since they're the only ones on that road and their home is unique, for lack of better words. Danielle has always been one to utilize everything around her and when you see her home, you'll understand what I mean."

"Wow, I can't even see their house from the road! They must be way back in the woods."

"Yup, and that's just the way they like it. They both really like the privacy that their place affords them and if my calculations are correct, our turn should be right about," he quickly yanked the steering wheel in a hard right, "here," he said as he turned onto a dirt drive almost hidden by overgrown shrubs.

"Holy shit," Nicole exclaimed as they slowly made their way down the very narrow drive, that reminded her more of a footpath than an actual driveway.

"I thought we got rid of these types of roads when we left the Lodge!" A second later, the driveway ended, and in front of them was their new home. Nicole's first impression was that it looked like Grandma's cabin in Little Red Riding Hood, with its' overgrown vines and thick forest encroaching on the yard. Then she spied the ornate bark covered flower boxes affixed below the windows with the remnants of what had probably been a beautiful cornucopia of seasonal flowers. Glancing in between the two windows facing the drive was a huge bird feeder and two very tiny and delicate looking hummingbird feeders. The sight of them made her smile and she knew that if the previous occupant had taken the time to plant flowers and feed the wildlife, then she felt confident that the inside would be well maintained and loved, like the exterior had obviously been at some point. Aedan put the truck into park and Nicole quickly exited. opened the doors for two whining dogs that were loudly announcing that they wanted their freedom from the confinement of the rear seat. The second they were out, they took off together bounding from tree to tree, sniffing and peeing, sniffing and peeing until it appeared that they'd hit every tree in the immediate vicinity. Just as Nicole was about to call them back, they came running at the sound of a truck engine as it got louder coming down the drive. Coming into view was Danielle's truck with Bruce riding shotgun. Both grinned and waved as soon as they made eye contact with Nicole, and then Aedan, who came to her side, putting his arm around her subconsciously as he watched his sister approach. Once parked, Danielle practically jumped out of the truck and into the waiting arms of her brother, her twin, and still her best friend in the world. She loved Bruce her fiancée with her heart and soul, but her twin brother was like an extension of herself. Every time she thought back to how close she'd coming to losing him last year, it made her physically sick to her stomach. Now here he was, moving in less than a mile from her own home, and he not only looked physically healthy, but had the look of someone in love. And the thought couldn't make her happier. From the second she'd met Nicole, something in her gut told her that not only was Nicole perfect for her brother, but also that she and Aedan needed each other and that neither would be complete without the other. Now, if only her hardheaded brother could figure it out on his own, she thought. Seeing him here, attached to Nicole's side made her eyes well up with tears. She saw that now, finally, they were a unit. Her beloved brother finallyhad someone to complete him. Taking them both into a bear hug, she pulled them in tight and smiled, laughed and cried all at the same time. She was so glad to have her brother back home and now living close by with Nicole and their menagerie of animals. Once the initial greetings were over, Danielle brought Nicole into the cabin to show her around as the men stayed outside untying the massive tarp covering their belongings. Nicole was immediately drawn to the open floor plan of the tiny cabin that seemed to allow one living space to lead into the other. The kitchen was cozy but appeared to have all the necessary accoutrements to make a gourmet meal. Nicole originally had some preconceived ideas about what her new kitchen might look like since the cabin was run solely on alternative power.   Having never utilized nontraditional utilities before, she wasn't sure what to expect. Now standing here, she realized that although it was very small, the kitchen in front of her looked no different than any other kitchen except that it lacked a dishwasher. Walking to the under mount farm style kitchen, she took a moment to look outside and gasped at the view. She couldn't believe it but it reminded her so much of their cabin in Maine. She saw nothing but woods, water and mountains from where she was standing and that made her smile. Then to her left of their property, she saw not only a huge greenhouse, but also a massive windmill. Turning back toward Danielle, she shrugged her shoulders and confessed to knowing little to nothing about either.

"Don't worry about it Nicole. Aedan and grew up with a greenhouse that our parents always use, he even designed and made one for us when we were kids so he's got that covered for you. Practically everyone up here uses wind power, water power or solar power so we can help you out with that as well. You treat your appliances in your home like you would any other conventional type home, you just have to be a little more conservative and aware of how many you're using at the same time. How about we get you settled, and then we'll give you a little tutorial on alternative energy," she said, smiling.

"God, I'm so glad you've brought my brother home to me," she said, smiling. "And I have you to thank for making him happy again; so for that, Thank You Nicole," she said, warmly as she put her arm around her waist.

"Come on, let's help them unload and then head back to my place for lunch and a few beers. Deal?"

"Deal."

They didn't have much to unload and with four of them, they had everything off the truck and inside the home within a half hour. Nicole insisted that they just simply leave everything in the living area and then go eat lunch as she was already famished. No one argued, and once they had everything unloaded, Aedan called Nicole's dogs inside so they could head over to his sister's place.

Nicole and Aedan decided to catch a ride with Danielle so that they could walk back to their cabin after lunch and get a feel for the land. It only took two minutes by truck to reach Danielle and Bruce's drive, which both Aedan and Bruce were thankful since Nicole and Danielle talked continuously the entire ride. Once the truck came to a stop, Nicole was in awe of what lay in front of her. Danielle had stated that she and Bruce lived in a modest little home on the outskirts of town. But he had failed to mention that it appeared to be comprised of entirely recycled materials. When she took a closer look, she saw that no two windows were the same size, part of the home was made of wood, part was stucco and the remaining appeared to be white brick. The ornate entrance was guarded by two gargoyles set atop concrete pedestals directly in front of massive log pillars holding up a covered porch complete with burgundy colored clay shingles. Before entering their home, Nicole stood on the landing admiring the intricate stained glass window in the wooden front door. Lost in thought, Nicole jumped when Aedan came up behind her and wrapped his arms around her waist.

"Pretty fancy huh? Bruce is a huge brut of a man, but he loves designing stained glass masterpieces. He designed and made that door for Danny when he moved in with her. Wait until you see some of the pieces scattered throughout their home," he added. Suddenly self-conscious of Aedan's open display of affection, Nicole stepped forward and out of his embrace and into Danielle's home.

She wasn't sure how she felt about the menagerie of materials that encompassed the exterior of Danielle's home but the second she entered the two story foyer, she nearly gasped at the view. Her first thought was even though it was somewhat overcast outside, the house was so bright and seemed to welcome the outdoors in. The entire rear of the cabin was made of glass and with skylights above, the room gave the appearance of still being outside. The cabin's wooden walls were stained a light shade of gray which made the room look much grander than the actual square footage. Nicole's first impression was that Danielle and Bruce's taste was definitely ecliptic as she viewed the room and the mismatch of styles, prints and woods that she saw in the compact great room. Then her eyes honed in on the large canvas print hung proudly about their fire place mantel. She walked silently toward the stone wall, never wavered her stance from the print hanging proudly about the wood stove.

"That painting," she asked, spellbound. "Where did you get it? It's absolutely amazing!"

Before Danielle could get Aedan's attention and answer, he answered Nicole's question for his sister.

"Oh that old thing. Didn't some guy give that to you back when you were just a kid," he asked nonchalantly." Danielle looked at him slightly confused but seeing his facial expression, she suddenly understood.

"Oh yeah. That was given to me when I was like 17 or 18. Kept telling him how talented he was and that he should pursue his love of painting but he blew me off. If I remember correctly, that guy was really stubborn back then and still is for that matter."

"So you are still in touch with him? I've never seen anyone capture the true essence of the blood moon the way this painter did. I have absolutely no artistic ability and would love to meet him sometime to maybe commission him to do another one like this. I'm mesmerized by the size and mystique of a bull moose and I have an abnormal obsession with gray timber wolves," she chuckled, "but pictures and paintings of full moons absolute fascinate me! I love to sit outside under the full moon every month, whether its winter, spring, summer or fall. I've done it for years and a true blood moon is such a rare occurrence, and that artist got it exactly right. So after we get settled, do you think you could give me his information Danielle?"

Looking at her brother, she nodded and smiled before answering.

"Yeah sure Nic, I believe I can track him down and I think you'll really be intrigued by him. Don't you think Nicole will like him Aedan?" she asked her brother sarcastically.

Giving her a quick dirty look, he answered her pointed question.

"You always said that the artist who did that print is one very talented guy and if I remember correctly, you said he was not only talented but gorgeous. And one of the best looking starving artists ever," he said, trying to conceal his laughter.

"Jesus Christ it's getting deep in here," Bruce interjected. "It is an awesome print, but let's not get carried away here. He's not that good looking."

Nicole listened to the banter going around as she continued to look at the massive print depicting a full blood moon rising high above a serene looking lake with a tiny cabin nestled between the pines. The detailing in the print was impressive and seemed to tell a story of its' own. She looked at the three of them and asked, "Am I missing something here? You three seem to be in on some inside joke that I'm not privy to, so spill it. What don't I know about this artist?"

"Oh relax honey. There's nothing to tell about him. Just a guy who used to put his emotions on print and also happened to be fixated with full moons when he was a kid. Let me show you Danny's kitchen and let's get some of that beer that she promised us," he said, changing the subject.

"Okay. But I really want a print like that someday Aedan." She followed Aedan into the kitchen adjacent to the great room. Her eyes widened when she saw that Bruce and Danielle were also living off the grid and utilizing solar power and wind power, but their kitchen spared no amenity. She first noticed the stainless appliances that were a bold contrast to the black granite flooring and white cabinetry. The Carrera marble countertops were the perfect complement to blend the dark with the light. She appreciated the clean lines and vast amounts of countertop space, two things her tiny kitchen did not have. But beggars can't be choosers, she thought to herself and quickly redirected her attention back to Danielle.

"Wow Danielle, this is amazing. I absolutely love your kitchen," she said sincerely. "Did you design this too?"

"Actually yes. I gutted and rebuilt this kitchen myself, with a little help from one of the local carpenters," she responded, proudly.

"It is an accomplishment that I'm very proud of. Aedan isn't the only one with hidden talents," she winked, as she opened the fridge and motioned for Nicole to help herself to a cold beer, while Aedan did the same.

They all grabbed their favorite beverage and then Danielle continued their two second tour. She showed them the two cozy bedrooms and bath on the main living level and then proceeded to have them make their way downstairs. Having their home built on a slope afforded them the ability to not only have large windows in the basement but also walk out atrium doors leading to the back yard. As Nicole was admiring the views, Aedan pulled Bruce aside and had a private conversation that the girls weren't privy to. After a few minutes, the four of them made their way upstairs and sat down to enjoy the meal that Danielle had prepared for the four of them. They laughed and talked during the entire meal and

Danielle kept looking at her brother and his interaction with Nicole. She felt that her heart grew ten sizes when she realized that she'd been absolutely right about her brother's feelings.

Danielle answered Nicole's barrage of questions thrown at her about her town, the community and the make-up of the people both in town and on the outskirts of town. Danielle described what a tight knit, hardworking blue color type community she lived in. Bruce interjected that many of the men in the immediate area either worked at the lumber yard, at Wilson International, on their own independent farms, or out of town during the week, faithfully returning on weekends. Danny added that the town was relatively self-sufficient and now that they had medical staff again, they truly didn't need any outside influence. When Nicole asked what Danielle meant about the town not needing outside influence, Danielle was polite but vague, simply stating that their little town prided itself on not needing help from the government, corporate conglomerates or outsiders. Danielle went on to say that even though Aedan and Nicole were coming to fill a gap in their tiny infrastructure; she forewarned them not to be surprised if people were slightly standoffish and reserved at first. Danielle explained that her town was comprised of some of the most hardworking, honest, god-fearing people she'd ever met, but they were sometimes very leery of change and outsiders and might take just a little bit of time to warm up to them. Nicole thought about what Danielle was implying and though she had worded her responses sensitively, Nicole couldn't help but get the feeling that there was something about the townsfolk that Danielle wasn't telling her.

"Oh well," she thought to herself, "I'm here now so it's a little too late to worry about any small town paranoia or quirkiness."

When they'd finished lunch, Aedan and Nicole thanked his sister and future brother-in-law and said their goodbyes as they explained that they needed to take the afternoon to get settled and unpack what little they'd brought. Danielle offered to bring all of Aedan's winter attire that she'd had stored in her basement, over in the morning as she was still washing it since it'd been in storage for years. Nicole then remembered that she'd used Danielle and Bruce's mailing address for her things that Gwen, her best friend, had packed up for her and was shipping via UPS. Thinking back now, she'd probably had Gwen over pack for her but since she really had no idea what to expect during a true New England winter, she had relayed to her best friend that more was probably better than less. And knowing Gwen, she'd probably receive a truckload of boxes! Nicole told Danielle that her shipment would probably arrive on Monday while she was at the clinic for the first time, and if it did, just to let her know and they'd swing by on their way back from work. All agreed and with that, Aedan and Nicole set off on foot to return to their dogs and their new home.

Chapter 11

So used to having Neiko forever present during her walks, Nicole actually felt slightly awkward being truly alone with Aedan as they walked down his sister's long drive and on to the road connecting their properties. The silence afforded her the time to relive the scenario that she'd instigated in her truck on their way out of the lodge. She wasn't sure what had gotten into her, and though she didn't necessary regret it, she did, in fact, feel a little embarrassed by her lack of constraint. Aedan on the other hand, was also thinking about that sudden, surprising chain of events and was hoping and praying that it wasn't a one-time occurrence. They made small talk as they walked, with Nicole forever looking for signs of moose. He chuckled when he thought of her obsession with the ugly looking creature, but if it made her smile and happy, then he'd spend the rest of his days in search of them too. They laughed together at Nicole's reaction to how eclectic and unique Danielle's home is and Aedan went on to explain that Danielle had been like a vagabond, so to speak, after finishing college. While some college kids set off for Europe to sightsee, Danielle had, against his advice and better judgment, had done something very similar to what Nicole had. She set off for parts unknown, by herself, with no destination in mind. She had wound up in this little New England town, which was no more than a blip on a map, and never left. After she'd traveled up and down the entire east coast, Aedan hadn't realized at first what had drawn his twin sister to put down roots here, in a one horse town without so much as a red-light or Dunkin Donuts in it. But after spending almost all of his time while on leave with his sister, the town and its inhabitants had grown on him, and he had come to discover what his sister had known from the start. Now here he was, with someone he truly loved, putting down the closest thing he'd ever had to roots.

Once back at their cabin, they took a few minutes to allow the dogs to go out and relieve themselves, and used the opportunity to check out the back yard and river. While Nicole went straight to the water's edge, Aedan wandered towards the old greenhouse to see if it was salvageable. From the angle that he walked to the greenhouse, he had to push several blown down branches away to even gain access. Aedan doubted that the structure would have any redeeming value but at least it he might be able to reuse some of the materials. Once the door was pried open, he gazed inside and felt like he had walked into some type of time warp. How could this be possible he thought as he gazed inside? From the outside, it had looked like a broken down, haphazardly built structure, but once inside, he saw that it was full of vegetables of every shape and size, trees with blooming fruits visible on their branches, pods of strawberries and blueberries and blackberries, and hanging walls of gourds and cucumbers. He'd never seen anything like it before and couldn't comprehend what it was doing here, behind an abandoned log cabin. As he walked up and down the makeshift isles, he took note of the too numerous to count types of vegetables. He opened his phone, still mesmerized, and called his sister. Before she could even say hello, he blurted out, "Danny, who the hell's been keeping up the greenhouse? It's amazing! And am I responsible for it because I really don't think I'm going to have time between setting up the clinic and seeing patients all day, and then there's Nicki. I need time with her and the dogs and I just really don't think I know enough about greenhouses to maintain something as intricate as this one." And at that moment, when Aedan had finally stopped talking, Danielle burst out laughing, genuinely laughing.

"What," he practically shouted.

"You," she exclaimed. "You've become just like Nicole; where you can talk for a minute straight, and ask about five things at once, all in one breathe. It's like you two are already an old married couple," she teased.

"In answer to your questions, I and some of the locals and tribeswomen take care of it so you won't have to worry about maintaining anything but the clinic. And Aedan, you're going to have to tell her soon you know. I don't honestly expect that Nicki will actually meet some of our more remote neighbors but she needs to know that they exist Aedan. Occasionally some of them come to our side of the river and help Monica, Nadine and I in the greenhouse. They truly have been a wonderful asset and their knowledge is endless you know. I wish we knew half as much as they do about working with nature."

"I know Danny, I will. I just don't want to overload her that's all. She's tough as nails you know, and really intelligent. But I just want to try and ease her into this new environment and new job and not freak her out about how eccentric some of the backwoods folks can be."

"Eccentric, yeah okay, right; that's what they are. Okay, you do what you think is best. You know her better than I do. Call me if you want to come back tonight for dinner okay?"

"Okay Danny, and thank you. Thank you for welcoming her into your home and our family."

"Oh shit Aedan that parts easy. You love her so we, Bruce and I, in turn love her. She's an extension of you now Aedan. You two are two parts of a unit and that is how you're meant to be. She's your soulmate stupid and it's about time that you figured that out. We did the second we met her. I just have one request big brother," she added.

Stunned by what his sister had said, she simply asked "What   is   that   Danny?" "Promise me that you won't marry her before Bruce and I finally get around to tying the knot!"

"What? I have no intention," he said indignantly "of marrying Nicole or anyone else for that matter, anytime soon."

Chuckling, she simply said, "Yeah right," and hung up.

Chapter 12

Nicole and Aedan rearranged the cabin, unpacked their belongings and took stock of what they had on hand, while Nicole made a list of what they'd need in town. They had the music cranked on the ancient boom box that they had found in a kitchen cupboard, which surprisingly still had batteries that were good. Nicole remained very nervous about the concept of alternative energy while the thought didn't bother Aedan in the least. As she continued to unpack her most cherished possessions, she took a second to sit down on what would be her bed, and removed her beloved, and very worn guitar from its' case. She strummed a few cords and then stopped as quickly as she had picked it up. She carried her guitar out the atrium doors that were in her bedroom and walked slowly down to the river. She sat at the river's edge and just looked out at the incredible beauty that surrounded her as her dogs took their positions as if they were sentries standing guard of their master. She started playing what was in her heart. Aedan watched her from the kitchen as she and her dogs wandered away from the cabin but left her alone in her thoughts; knowing that she usually played her guitar when she needed to work things through in her head. So he let her be.

She quickly became lost in her music and daydreams as she played. Though the current of the river behind her new home wasn't half the velocity of the Western River she'd left behind in Maine, its movement and rhythm soothed her just the same. She listened to the current as it bubbled while making its' passage downstream. Opening her eyes, she caught a movement out of the corner of her eye. Across the river, something had moved but she couldn't see anyone or anything now. Not at all alarmed, she just assumed it was a deer or could have been a bear for that matter. She continued playing for another few minutes while occasionally sneaking a peak across the river. Nothing else caught her attention as she played and she quickly forgot about whatever had moved, assuming that it was just some kind of wild animal. After a few more minutes, feeling refreshed, she got up and started heading back toward the cabin where Aedan was waiting patiently for her.

"Hey," he said nonchalantly when she entered the cabin.

"Hey yourself. Sorry, I took a little breather and went for a walk down by the river. You get your stuff unpacked" she asked somewhat nervously. Before he even had a chance to answer, she continued. "I am pretty well unpacked, at least as much as I can be until I get my winter gear that Gwen mailed. So I was thinking about heading back into town to grab more groceries. I know we have all weekend but no time like the present right so

I thought I'd go for a ride. You have anything in particular that you'd like me to pick up?"

Sensing that she wanted to make the trek into town alone, Aedan didn't react. "Well, maybe just the basics would be fine to start with. Maybe milk, eggs, bread, and coffee? Please get coffee," he laughed. "It's going to be a reality check getting back onto a real schedule again. You go in to town whenever you're ready and I'll take care of the boys while you're gone. Is it okay if I bring them with me back over to Danny's? Bruce wanted me to come over when I had an hour to spare, and like you said, there's no time like the present," he smiled. Thinking he was acting somewhat peculiar, she now wished she'd asked him to join her as she knew that he absolutely would if she had asked. But too late for that now.

"Oh, okay. I shouldn't be more than an hour or so. So I guess I'll see you and the boys later," she said, patting her leg to call her dogs over.

"You two be good for Aedan," she said, crouching down to their eye level and kissing them both on their noses, as if they understood what she was saying. Standing back up, she finished her sentence.

"You sure you're okay with them Aedan," she asked, now slightly nervous, somehow knowing he was up to something but not sure what. What could Bruce need him for already, since they had just spent a few hours over there earlier today, she wondered?

He leaned into her and quickly gave her a peck on the cheek.

"We'll be good honey, don't worry about us Nic. Oh, and could you maybe pick up a 12 pack of Labatt's Blue for me, and a nice bottle of white wine?" he asked with a sly grin.

"I'll take care of supper this evening if you'll grab the booze. Oh, and maybe a bottle of Winter Jack or Petron, or both," he winked.

Now absolutely sure that he was up to something, she simply nodded and smiled and walked out the door to her truck.

As soon as Nicole left, Aedan called his sister quickly and told her he'd be right over, declining her offer of a ride. He grabbed the dog's leashes, just in case he needed them, and headed out the door with the two shepherds in tow. He, like Nicole, walked at an extremely brisk pace so it only took a few minutes to reach his sister's driveway. As he walked, his mind was racing as he planned out the evening. He didn't have all of the details worked out quite yet, but he wanted more than anything for their first night together in their new home to be not only romantic but a night neither one of them would forget. He wanted it to be special and wanted Nicole to feel at home and have no regrets about her decision to try this new endeavor. And very selfishly, he thought that if she wanted to go another round like they had in her truck earlier that morning, that'd be okay as well. Hell, one can only hope and pray, he thought to himself as he walked into his sister's home, dogs in tow.

"Hey honey, where are you? Danny? Bruce?" he called out. Not hearing them, he went back outside and around the side of their home and towards Bruce's pole barn. Hearing the music as he turned the corner, the dogs raced towards the barn. Ten seconds later, he heard his sister hollering at the dogs to leave the chickens alone, and not chase the goats. He burst out laughing at the swear words coming out of his sister's mouth as he entered the barn. There, sitting innocent looking were Nicole's two dogs, the younger one with remnants of a few feathers still in his mouth.

"Sorry Danny," he said, still chuckling. "The boys here aren't used to farm animals quite yet. Doubt Nicki had any when she lived in Syracuse and we certainly didn't have any at the Lodge. Tell them NO sternly and they're really pretty damn smart so they'll leave your animals alone. Sinjin didn't get your chicken did he," he asked, swiping the feathers from the pup's mouth.

"No, he did not, luckily," she said, trying to sound exasperated but not being very convincing.

"Well that's good, then isn't it?" he said, and changed the subject. "Where is Bruce and my baby?"

"He's in back, with your baby; doing some last minute fine tuning. He said to not expect miracles since she's quite temperamental, and OLD," she teased. "Not nearly as fancy as your girlfriend's ride," she added to just to piss her brother off, knowing how much he loved his truck.

"She may be slighter older than Nicole's truck, but I'll have you know," he said, trying to sound indignant, "that she's not old, she's classic and once she's up and running, she's more refined than all of those new trucks out there on the road. They don't make them like they did when she came out."

"And I thank God for that nightly! Aedan, you do realize that your truck was assembled years before we were even born right? You're a doctor you know. I bet you could afford something a little newer and maybe now that you're gonna be stateside permanently, and living up here where we get A LOT of snow, you should seriously consider looking into getting a better, more dependable set of wheels. I know you love Maude and all, but seriously Aedan..."

"She'll be fine Danielle, she'll be fine," he said as he made his way to the rear of the pole barn in search of Bruce and a certain blue Ford F-250. He found them both and smiled.

Chapter 13

Nicole pulled into the parking lot of the local grocery store and silently thanked God that although the town was relatively small in size, they still had a chain grocery store. She had absolutely nothing against small town mom and pop type grocery stores but since she did in fact love to bake, she was pleased to see a larger store and hopefully that meant a big selection inside to help her get a jump start on filling her pantry. She's been pleasantly surprised when she and Aedan had discovered that her pantry had already been partially stocked with essentials by Aedan's sister. But Danielle had inadvertently forgotten many key food staples that both she and Aedan couldn't live without. Grabbing a grocery cart and heading inside, she was greeted by the warm smile of a teenager attending to the recycling center.

"Good afternoon mam. Welcome to Everest." Somewhat taken back by the friendly welcome, Nicole smiled back. "Good afternoon to you as well," reading his name tag, she added "Ted". "Does everyone get greeted with such a warm welcome when they come in to do a little shopping" she asked.

"Oh course mam. We welcome everyone mam, especially new folks to the area."

Now curious, she studied the young man standing in front of her that she estimated was probably 17 or 18. He was a very handsome teenager, with strikingly black hair and the darkest brown eyes she'd ever seen. His olive skin tone and high cheek bones gave him a very European or Middle Eastern appearance. She quickly noted his hands as they were calloused and looked like they should belong to an individual three times his age. His statute was tall and proud as he stood as if guarding the recycling center as if his life depended on it. She thought even with his warm welcome, his eyes looked somewhat weary.

"What makes you think I'm new to the area?"

He stalled for just a second or two before answering.

"I saw you this morning when you were driving through town and you and the man you were with stopped in front of our hospital. Out of state tags, and we were expecting the Doc to arrive soon, so it didn't take much to put two and two together mam."

"I wouldn't exactly call it a hospital Ted," she stammered, still slightly skeptical of his astute observation.

"With all due respect mam, in our eyes, it's all we need up here. And we're all thankful that you and the doc came. Some of the townsfolk will take a little getting used to, and some will be reluctant in trusting you since you aren't from here. But give them time and they'll come around," he smiled. "I'll let you get shopping. If there's anything that you can't find, you can have someone page me and I'll help you out okay?" Before she could answer, he turned and disappeared around the corner and out of sight.

"Okay," she thought to herself and pushed her cart inside.

Just as she had expected, the store was a cornucopia of items ranging from the basic staples to some very usual and exotic notions and food options, some of which she'd never even heard of before. They had herbs and spices that she was vaguely familiar with but had never cooked with before and the fresh fruit, even this late in the growing season was diverse and looked very appealing. The selection the store offered was exemplarily in Nicole's eyes. She quickly filled her cart and thought it best to check out before she got too carried away. Having picked up enough to fill their pantry, refrigerator and most of the freezer, Nicole felt confident that they now had everything they'd need to carry them over for the next few weeks. Besides, with the grocery store only four or five blocks from the clinic. If there was anything she'd forgotten or Aedan needed, one of them could simply walk over during their lunch hour.

"Aedan," she thought now, "How weird was it going to be to be working side by side with him every day and then going home with him in the evening?" Suddenly nervous, she stood in line at the checkout wondering what she was going to do with him. Here she was, living in a tiny town away from everything familiar to her, about to embark on a type of nursing that she'd never done before, with a man who was her roommate, her co-worker, and sort of her boss; and who, after today's lack of inhibition, her lover.

"Oh my God," she thought to herself, feeling her face turning beet red, "I freaking jumped him like a wild teenager," she now realized and suddenly felt very embarrassed all over again. "And he didn't say a word to stop me!" thinking back to their little scenario in her truck. "And he never said a word about it afterwards, like it was an everyday occurrence for him! Pompous jackass," she thought now, shifting her embarrassment to lightning fast anger. Before her temper could spin into full blown rage, it was her turn to check out and she was greeted by an adorable, bubbly red headed young cashier.

"Hello, and welcome to Everest's. Did you find everything that you were looking for mam?"

"Yes I did, thank you," Nicole answered back, trying not to let her simmering temper show.

"Great, would you like some assistance out to your car this afternoon" she asked as her right hand scanned the items with exact precision and record speed.

"Um, no, I'll be fine, thank you." Momentarily distracted, Nicole genuinely smiled. "If everyone," she thought to herself, "is as friendly as the people in this store; working at the clinic should be a piece of cake." She finished paying as the red head kept on chatting. Looking up, she saw Ted rounding the corner and walking right up to her cart.

"Let me help you with these," he offered, taking ahold of her overflowing cart.

"Hey Mandy," he said, smiling at the gum snapping teenager who had cashed her out. "Did you meet the newest addition to our town? She's here to run the clinic," he said with great enthusiasm.

Feeling that she needed to be addressed by something other than "mam," she looked at the two teenagers and said, "Well now that I know both of your names, let me formally introduce myself since I'm too young to go by Mam," she teased. I'm Nicole Brentwood and yes, I'll be working with Doctor O'Bryan at the clinic. You can call me Nicole if you'd like. Mrs. Brentwood sounds too formal don't you think?" she smiled, at her new found friends.

Mandy snapped her gum one last time and held out her hand, "Officially welcome to Mystique. We're really glad you came Mam; I mean Nicole," she said, looking at Nicole with green eyes very similar in shade to her own.

"I'm here most afternoons and on Saturdays so if you need help finding something, you just holler."

"Thank You Mandy, I'll remember that," she said as they started walking out of the store and towards her truck. After Ted had helped her load bag after bag into the cab of her truck, she turned to offer him a few bucks for his trouble, which he prompted refused. Thanking him for his assistance, she waved as she started to pull out of the lot.

Her first encounter had gone very well and the kids had made her not only feel welcome but also at ease, at least at the moment. Now, she thought, she had to go back to the cabin and face him. And look at him knowing full well that she'd seduced him and jumped his bones just hours before. Feeling that she was getting all worked up again, she put in a Bob Segar CD and immediately started singing to get her mind off of the inevitable. She knew that she and Aedan would have to discuss what happened earlier, and he needed to understand that it wouldn't be happening again.

It only took a few minutes to be back on the road leading to her new home. Pulling into the drive, Nicole wondered who was visiting when she brought her truck to a stop beside a very shiny but ancient looking pick up. The front door opened almost immediately as if he'd been waiting for her, as Aedan and her dogs came bounding out. She took a few seconds to greet her best friends, and reached into her side panel to retrieve a few of the ever present dog treats. And then she looked into those damn light blue eyes of his and she was gone; again.

"Hey! Looks like you made a killing," he said, smiling just big enough to have his dimples come out full force.

Still finding it hard to make eye contact with him, she simply smiled back.

"Who's truck? We have company already," she asked as she loaded up her arms with the remaining bags.

"Nope," he said. "That's Maude, and she's mine," he shouted back as he entered the cabin, holding open the door for her as she quickened her pace to catch up.

Walking past him so that she could set the overload of bags down, she subconsciously put her hands on her hips and turned to face him.

"What do you mean she's yours? You went out and bought an antique truck while I was grocery shopping Aedan," she asked, somewhat confused.

"Not exactly. I've owned Maude since I was a freshman in college. I rebuilt her myself. I'll have to show you pictures sometime of what she looked like when I got her," he added.

"Okay. I assume that MAUDE was hanging out at Danielle and Bruce's and that's why you had to go over there today," she asked.

"Yup. I thought I should have my own set of wheels so we're not using your truck all the time. And I was hoping that maybe you'd like to go out on a date with me tomorrow evening Ms. Brentwood," he asked, with the sincerest tone she'd heard come out of his mouth in weeks.

"You want to take me out on a date Aedan," she asked, now very perplexed by his strange request. "I'd think," Nicole said tentatively, "that we're slightly past the first date arena, don't you think? Especially after this morning," she added, for effect.

"Nope Ms. Brentwood, I would be honored if you'd accompany me out tomorrow evening. Nothing elaborate since I plan on working you half to death tomorrow getting the clinic up and running during the day. But tomorrow evening, we'll go out on the town, and I'm driving and we're taking Maude. Deal?"

As much as she fought it, she melted as she peered into those amazing blue eyes. "Deal."

Chapter 14

They unloaded the numerous bags of groceries in relative silence. Aedan took direction from Nicole as to where to she wanted the various nonperishables placed. The dogs went between the two of them, always hopeful that a treat or two would find their way to the floor, and Aedan did not disappoint.

It was practically dinner time by the time they had their cozy cabin organized and tidied up and as much as Nicole just wanted to collapse in a chair on the patio and read, Aedan informed her that his sister had ordered pizza and wings and invited them to dinner. Seeing a less than excited expression come over her face, he quickly offered to run over to her house and just grab a few slices for them and bring them back. She knew that his sister was only trying to help so she put on her best game face and said she'd love to go over to Danielle and Bruce's, but not for the whole evening, she interjected. He agreed and handed her a glass of wine which she clanged against his Labatt's to seal the deal. She excused herself once she realized that they weren't due over at his sister's for another hour, explaining that she was dying for a bath in their claw foot bath tub. Neiko followed her into their bathroom but the pup stayed behind with Aedan. With time to kill, he decided to go back out to the greenhouse and take a closer look at the large variety of produce growing inside. Before heading out, he poked his head inside the tiny bath to let her know that he was taking Sinjin outside. He smiled to see her up to her chin in bubbles.

He whistled along the way as he and their pup walked outside and towards the enormous greenhouse. As they approached, he noted the fur rise on the puppy's back and heard a very low guttural growl emit from the dog's throat. Instantly on alert, he quickly proceeded to the greenhouse and silently slid inside. He knew that someone had just been inside the building, he could feel their presence, but whoever it was, was gone now. Nothing was disturbed nor out of place from what he could tell. But it still made him very uneasy that someone had just been that close to their cabin without him realizing it. Then he remembered what Danielle had said about several of the local women who tended to the greenhouse. And then he felt the tension ease from his shoulders and realized how silly he'd been. He obviously was becoming way too paranoid and he chastised himself for overreacting.

She hadn't been paying attention to her environment and surroundings and had almost gotten caught. Being seen was not an option. He would have punished her if she'd been caught in the greenhouse, and that thought alone terrorized her more than anything. He was a merciless disciplinarian and she feared his temper. Just out of sight, she squatted behind the large hemlock, panting from her 50 yard dash from the rear of the greenhouse. Sure, it was okay to be inside it with her mother, but she was forbidden to cross the river without her mother or brother present he'd said. But he wasn't her boss, she'd thought as she headed toward the area of the river downstream where it was shallow and narrow compared to behind the greenhouse. It wasn't like she was doing anything illegal, she'd thought to herself. She'd help plant many of those plants, had lovingly started them from seeds and alongside her mother, had tended to them, thinned them, watered them and picked their harvest throughout the summer. As she rested, out of sight, to catch her breath, she thought about the nice ladies from town that she'd met at the greenhouse. She really liked the lady with the blonde hair who always complained about tending to the garden plants, but was always inside. She knew that the blonde lad was always tenderly touching their leaves, and watering them and on more than one occasion, Rainie had caught her talking and singing to the seedlings. Most of the plants were products of pre-germination and propagation and some technology that she didn't quite understand. The pretty blonde lady and her mother would whisper back and forth as they worked on the seedlings like they knew some deep secret and it saddened her that they wouldn't reveal their magic to her, saying she was too young to understand. But she wasn't too young, and she would show them that she too could take two plants and make them one; she would study them and learn their ways, just like she'd learned so much from them already. The blonde that her mother called Danny was funny, she thought to herself. And she was so pretty. But now she wondered who the man and lady were that had moved into the cabin and if they would ruin it for her mother and she, since she loved crossing to their side of the river and spending time with the women from outside her village. Why hadn't their lady friend told her mother about the strangers? Or why hadn't Bruce since he seemed to be very close friends with her momma? The man had almost caught her inside, and what would he had done to her if she'd been caught? Maybe her father was right after all. Maybe they needed to keep their community separate from the townspeople. Well, she thought now, as she stared at the greenhouse and hadn't seen the man come back out, she'd wait and see. Maybe her father was right, but maybe he wasn't; times had changed and her family was no different than any of the other people in town, and she hated that her father and some of the other members of her community didn't trust anyone that wasn't like them. Her mother and she knew that there were good people in town, and not just in their secluded community. Knowing that soon she would be missed at home, she silently disappeared into the thicket of trees and out of sight.

Nicole chilled in the chest deep water with her glass of wine and her dog at her side. It felt great to relax in a bath with no one waiting for her to hurry up and finish, or expecting anything from her. As much as she was nervous about what Monday would have in store for her when she and Aedan opened the clinic, she was actually starting to get excited about the prospect of being a nurse again. It was in her blood to be a nurse, she thought to herself. Not having any children of her own, nursing afforded her an outlet in which to provide nurturing, caring and healing to people who needed it. She'd avoided that reality for too long. And now she was ready to tackle her new role head on. She finished up her wine and her bath as her dog slept beside the antique tub, snoring softly as he always did. She surveyed the tiny bath as she allowed the water to slowly drain out, and realized that it was about as perfect as it could be. Whoever had designed it, had done so as if they were designing it just for her. From the lacey white country curtains, to the draperies with their tiny lilac print that hung from a birch bark twig in front of the lone bay window, to the fresh vase of lavender beside the pedestal sink; the room was tastefully done, yet eloquent in its' own right. She grabbed her towel and stepped out onto the 18" rustic barn planks that covered the floor, and chuckled when a few drops of water dripped off her body and directly onto her sleeping pup's nose. Yes, she thought, now that she was refreshed and relaxed, this is a new chapter, a new beginning, and she was going to make the most of it.

Chapter 15

Aedan was curled up with a book when she entered the living room. He silently scanned the woman standing in front of him up and down, and nodded in approval. Nicole had decided that although this wasn't a date, they were simply going over to his sister's for pizza. There was no reason that she couldn't get a little dressed up. She hadn't really messed with her hair or makeup, since she wasn't really into painting on layers of the stuff, and preferred a more natural appearance. But she had taken the time to shave her legs, put on a light green sundress that accentuated her green eyes with the amazingly long eyelashes, and had pulled her hair up in a simple twist. Not one for much jewelry either, she'd only added a few bangle bracelets, and drop earrings that had always reminded her of moon beams. Wanting to break the silence, she twirled around and smiled.

"Don't stare at me Aedan! It's not like you've never seen me in a dress before." And then she remembered that the last time he'd seen her in a sundress, was the night when she'd been knocked out, kidnapped and would surely have died if not for the tenacity of her dog and Aedan.

He couldn't think of the right words for how amazing she looked, and how much he loved her. So he simply said, "You look stunning, absolutely radiant Nicole."

Now, very uncomfortable and blushing slightly, she knew that if they didn't go to his sister's immediately, they'd never make it. Shrugging his comments off, she smiled.

"Thanks Aedan. I'm ready if you are. So let's get going," she said, promptly walking past him and out the door. Turning back, "And don't forget to bring the bottle of wine I bought," she yelled back as she got into her truck so she could let her racing heart settle.

They headed over to Danielle and Bruce's and although they truly intended to just stay just long enough to avoid being rude, but found that they were having so much fun, they remained there drinking, eating and laughing for the next three hours. When they finally decided to leave, it was nearly ten. The pizza and wings were long gone, the wine Nicole had brought over, and the bottles Danielle had found were empty and the 12 pack of Blue was also empty. Feeling the buzz, Nicole didn't dare get behind the wheel, and Aedan felt about the same, so they accepted Bruce's offer of a ride. Being 6'5" and almost 250 pounds of pure muscle, Bruce didn't have nearly the buzz that the other three had. Aedan and Nicole promised to swing by first thing in the morning to pick up her truck which Bruce assured them was not a big deal, as they poured themselves out of his cab and headed towards their new cabin. Bruce waited for them to get inside, honked and drove back home to his waiting woman. If his hypothesis was right, all of them were in for a memorable evening and he wanted to get home post haste.

Once inside, Nicole called her dogs, let them out and kicked off her wedges as she waited until they came back in. Aedan wasn't under foot as she waited for her dogs to return, which gave her a moment to compose herself. Not sure where they were going from here, Nicole decided that maybe it was time to stop worrying about everything, stop trying to control the future, and just let fate intervene. She was not interested in finding another soulmate, she'd already had her one and only. Nor was she interested in getting married and having a family someday; that option died when her husband did. Aedan was a good man, she knew that now, and he had never pushed her or asked her to give more of herself than what she could. And for that fact alone, she loved him even more. But he was a man, and wouldn't be willing to wait around for her forever and she knew that they were at a pivotal point in their relationship.

"Well," she thought to herself as she continued to enjoy her very pleasant buzz. "Let's see how tonight is going to play out," and with that, she shut the door to the outside world and focused on what was inside and waiting for her.

She'd given him just enough time to wash up, brush his teeth and try and calm his nerves.

"This is so freaking ridiculous," he said under his breath. "It's not like I've never seen her naked before. And it's not like we've never had sex," he said, thinking back to their very spontaneous romp in her truck just this morning. "So why the hell is this woman making me so nervous, and have my hands sweating like a horny teenager?" He didn't need anyone to answer for him since he already knew that the answer was because none of the other woman who'd come before Nicole Rose had ever really mattered to him. And that thought terrified him all over again. He exited the bath just as she was entering the bedroom. Not sure what to expect, he simply looked at her and smiled, "Hey."

"Hey yourself," She sat down at the edge of the bed and looked up at the man standing before her, and gently padded the bed beside her. She asked him to sit down at her side. He did as she requested, and waited for her to speak. She stayed silent for just a moment, as if trying to formulate the correct words to say as she slid her hand into his. She slowly turned to him and simply spoke from the heart.

"I'm ready Aedan. I'm never going to forget Jared, and I know that you've never asked me to or expected me to; but I feel that I need to tell you that. He was my husband, my best friend and my soul mate and I loved him with all of my heart. But you also need to know that I thought when he died, I died as well. But I didn't Aedan. As much as I tried to stay closed off to the world, and shut down my feelings so that I could remain numb, I couldn't stay that way. And as much as I fought it, I have you to thank for that. You made me realize that I'm still alive, that I still can feel things other than pain and sorrow, and I can find happiness someday, and I have. I have with you Aedan."

She took a deep breath and continued, "I love you Aedan and it doesn't matter what the future holds in store for us, I just wanted to thank you for making me feel again, and for forcing me to live again."

Knowing that she was typically long winded and might ramble on for minutes, he grabbed her and brought his mouth to hers, finally squelching her dialogue. He felt her melt into the kiss and reach up and caress her fingers through the back of his hair, a move that turned him on immensely every time she did it. They continued locked in the embrace for what seemed like hours when he finally ended it. Still holding her, he was about to speak when she spoke first.

"Let's go to bed Aedan, and let's leave the dogs in the other room."

He didn't respond, he simply stood, left the room to lockup their cabin, gave each dog a treat, shut out the remaining lights and closed the door as he entered their bedroom. She too had dimmed the lights and in the soft candle light, he joined her in their bed and they became one.

Chapter 16

They worked together all weekend cleaning, organizing, rearranging and rearranging some more at the clinic. The previous doctor had utilized an archaic filing system which made no sense to Nicole, so along with Miranda, the former doctor's office manager, who'd stopped in early Saturday morning, and stayed with them throughout the day. They worked together helping the transition for both of them. The two women literally recoded and reorganized all of the patient's records. Nicole laughed as Miranda, a lifelong resident of Mystique couldn't pick up a chart without telling some type of story, antidote or intriguing fact about each patient. They weeded out the charts that should have been closed out long ago at the time that the patient expired or relocated out of the area. That act alone eliminated over 20% of the files, much to Nicole's relief. She tagged the inside of the charts with Miranda's very helpful memos about each individual, and as the day wore on, she began to feel as if she was becoming part of this tight knit community. Here, in this little mountain side town, tucked between a vast mountain ridge, and a river vital to everyone's existence, there was no vast division of the masses. Everyone was essentially middle class, hardworking and just trying to survive and thrive as individuals, as families and as part of a community. From the information Miranda had provided, and the haphazard but quite extensive notes the former physician had dictated, it appeared that the townsfolk of Mystique, New Hampshire were a very hardy, self-sufficient lot. What was surprising to Nicole was the fact that everyone seemed to have some key contribution that made the community stronger. For what she could tell from the files in front of her and Miranda's comments, everyone worked or attended school. There was no mention in any of the files of generational welfare recipients who knew how to milk the system instead of earning their keep. It was obvious that some people had more influential jobs than others, but each and every one of the residents in this little town contributed to making the town what it was, self-contained and self-sufficient. Miranda boasted that most of the townsfolk were second or third generation and most had no intention of ever leaving. She herself was born in the farm house that she and her husband now shared, and would never leave the area. Miranda continued on, frankly stating that if something happened to their world outside of Mystique, she, like most of the town would be ready and able to sustain the way of life that she was accustomed to living. Not quite sure what she meant by her statement, Nicole just smiled and attributed her proclamation to someone priding themselves on being hardy and self-sufficient, and didn't attempt to read anything else into her generic statement, such as it was. When Miranda appeared to be done talking, both attempted to finish the arduous task of creating a more efficient filing system.

The weekend flew by and whether or not they were ready, Monday morning arrived and both she and Aedan were up before dawn to start their new adventure. Danielle had already called before they'd left for town, reassuring Nicole that she and Bruce would take care of her dogs and not to worry about them. She'd also given her brother one more word of encouragement, knowing how hard it was going to be for both he and Nicole to face their fears and ease back into medicine again. After hanging up the phone, Danielle silently prayed that their first day was quiet so that neither got overwhelmed or shell shocked.

Once they arrived at the clinic, they were greeted by a smiling Miranda, Deanna and Jeremiah who were all waiting inside as they pulled in the drive behind the old Victorian. Coming from the west, Aedan hadn't driven past the stately looking front of the home so had no idea what awaited them. They had another quick question and answer session with the staff and all took a deep breath as Jeremiah went outside to switch the closed sign over, indicating they were ready for business. Nicole turned to Aedan and feeling her own queasy stomach, smiled at him.

"We probably won't even have too many people coming in right? Probably most folks don't even know the clinic is open again, don't you think?" she asked, hoping for reassurance.

Hearing her question as he reentered the clinic, the lanky looking tech coughed gently to get her attention. "Um, I wouldn't necessarily bank on that mam, I mean Nicole," he corrected. He didn't need to explain himself as she watched the slow but steady stream of men, women and children filing into the waiting room.

"And we're off," she thought, jumping right into what she did best.

The day flew by for all as they treated cuts and bumps, sprains and viruses; and by days' end, Nicole could have sworn that they'd taken care of half the town. Some came out of curiosity, some came just to welcome them, and some came because there finally was a doctor in town and though he was not a local, his sister was, so by default he was as well. They welcomed their new doctor and nurse with restraint, but most were friendly and some came with handpicked, and store bought bouquets, and a few came with pies, while others came with baskets of freshly picked vegetables that were clearly harvested just that morning, and she and Aedan now had enough eggs to last a month. Nicole didn't have time to worry about if she was dictating or coding the visits correctly, she could figure that part out with Miranda later. For now, she was just doing what she did best, which was taking care of people who needed her. Though she and Aedan had never worked together in this capacity before, they got into a rhythm before days' end and it was evident, that whether they were at a lodge in the mountains of Maine or running a little clinic in the mountains of New Hampshire, they were in sync with one another. The two of them not only worked well with one another, but complimented each other beautifully. Where Aedan was more reserved and serious, Nicole radiance and genuine friendliness was able to make even the quietest, wariest little girl who came in to be seen, comfortable and laughing before she left, prescription in hand for the drugstore. They were a team, and it showed.

After the last patient had left, the five of them all but collapsed into the waiting room chairs. Each had their own opinions of how the day had gone, and each took turns sharing those opinions. Miranda, serious by nature, offered compliments regarding their care of her friends and neighbors, but was quick to say that as the billing coordinator, they'd have to fine tune their descriptions of services rendered a little clearer. As if being scolded by someone's mother, both Nicole and Aedan nodded in agreement. Deanna and Jeremiah were quick to jump in congratulating them on a very successful first day. Everyone said their good byes and Nicole couldn't wait to get home to her dogs as this was the first time in months that she'd been away from Neiko for any period of time. And quite frankly, she was anxious to take her shoes off and have a big, no make that, a huge glass of wine. The day had been successful, like her staff had said, but she was exhausted and was definitely not used to being on her feet for that many continuous hours. Sure, she'd done it all the time back at the hospital, but now, that seemed like light years away and only a distant memory. Once they locked up for the night, Aedan and Nicole quickly made their way to her truck and back to their cabin. The second they entered the cabin, the smell hit them. Nicole went immediately over to the stove, the source of the smell and inhaled deeply after cracking the oven door.

"Lasagna," Nicole thought, "Oh my God, Danielle brought us Lasagna, and garlic bread," she shouted to Aedan who was letting the two whimpering dogs out.

"Yeah, I know Nic," he shouted back. "She texted me at the clinic today and said that she was going to drop some off, but to reassure you that she wouldn't be invading our space and that tonight's the last free meal," he laughed. "Oh, and she said that there's a bottle of wine chilling next to an antipasto that she made for us as well. And lastly, she said to tell you, that there are two cannoli's in the refrigerator for dessert but for us to not get too used to that kind of dessert," he added.

Once the dogs were back inside and giving Nicole their undivided attention, Aedan excused himself to go change. Nicole played with both dogs for several minutes, who were just as excited to see her as she was them. Once they finally settled down, she met Aedan in the living room and exchanged smiles as she went in for her turn to change into something more relaxing. Once changed, she rejoined him in the tiny dining area where he had carried in the meal for the two of them. Sitting down at the table, she looked over at her two pets. The dogs had food in their respective bowls but weren't touching it until Nicole gave them the okay. She gave her approval and both dogs dug in. Pouring both she and Aedan a glass of wine, they clanked their glasses together

"Here's to a successful first day," she said, raising her glass to his.

"Absolutely. Cheers, you rocked it today."

"Thanks Aedan."

That simple, their lives together had thankfully become a simple balancing act of checks and balances and slowly but surely, they were getting used to their routine together. Sure they had spent the entire summer essentially together but here, without Andrew and Maria and the continuous flow of visitors, along with the other staff at the lodge, they truly felt like it was just the two of them. Fearing it would be awkward, both were relieved as how easy a transition it really had been.

Following dinner, and with more than an hour left of daylight, Nicole asked Aedan if he wanted to go for a quick run. Mentally exhausted, he politely declined but insisted that she bring Neiko with her, even though they were now living much closer to civilization than they were in Maine. Having intended on bringing her dog and her new puppy anyway, she quickly agreed. Neiko didn't require a leash on the country roads that she'd be jogging along, but having had very little time to work with her newest addition, Aedan's birthday gift to her, she reached for his leash and a handful of treats before taking off, with two dogs in tow.

She watched the pretty lady that now lived in the cabin take off down the road with two of the cutest puppies that she'd ever seen. The big one she knew was a German shepherd and he stayed right at the lady's side, never wavering from the pace that she was setting. The smaller one, on the other hand, didn't seem to like being on a leash and was fighting it and the pretty lady, as they made their way down the road and away from her. She stayed in the concealment of the forest until she was sure that they were gone and only then did she slowly, silently start her way towards the greenhouse. It wasn't fair, she thought to herself, that she couldn't come over and see how her plants were growing. How could they expect her beautiful plants to grow if no one was talking to them the way she and her mother had all these weeks. She moved toward the rear entrance of the green house, constantly searching for any sign of the man or any of the other neighbors for that matter. As quietly as she moved, she entered the greenhouse silently as well. She made it just one step inside before the arm came around her neck and the hand covered her scream.

Chapter 17

For being so young, she fought wildly; first biting him, and hurling her weight and elbow into his gut, nearly breaking his grip. He spun her around and grabbed both of her shoulders and shook her to get her attention.

"Stop it. Stop it now! I'm not going to hurt you," he practically screamed at the shaking girl. Hearing what he said after he kept repeating it, she looked up and into his eyes and into his soul, knowing that he meant what he said.

Once he realized that she wasn't fighting to break free any longer, he kept his hands still firmly planted on shoulders but repeated in a much quieter more neutral tone, "I am not going to hurt you."

He kept his eyes firmly fixed on the young terrified looking girl.

"I am going to remove my hands now and I don't expect you to run because I have no intention of having to chase you, do you understand me?"

He looked down at the young girl, child really, who was staring back up at him with a look of bold defiance and if not for her quivering lip giving her away, he would have expected her to bolt the second that he released his grasp. Slowly he removed one hand and then the second when she made no attempt to run. Looking at her now, it was as if she were no longer afraid, but actually challenging him by being there. He calculated that she couldn't be much older than nine or ten. Yet here she was, alone in his greenhouse, or the greenhouse that was located on the property that he was renting, to be exact. She continued scowling at him, but remained silent. It would be up to him to break the silence and try and figure out who she was and what she was doing inside the greenhouse without supervision.

"Who are you and what are you doing in my greenhouse?"

No response.

"What is your name, and how old are you little girl? You really shouldn't be out here by yourself this close to dark? Where are your parents and do you want me to call them to come and get you?"

No response.

Becoming frustrated by her stubbornness and beginning to worry that Nicole hadn't returned from her run yet, Aedan tried to intimidate the stubborn girl by crouching down eye level with her as she stood there, straight as a rod with her arms crossed in front of her with sealed lips. Her eyes appeared unwavering but what Aedan didn't realize was that she had taken in everything that she could about the very tall man currently standing nose to nose with her. He knew from her appearance that she must be part Native American as her hair couldn't be any blacker and was long and straight and had the most beautiful sheen to it, reminding him of black ivory. Her cheekbones set high on her face and even though she were still just a child, anyone could see by studying her facial features that she was going to grow up to be stunningly beautiful. But for right now, she was slightly dirty, slightly mad, and very stubborn.

Now just inches from her face, he spoke as calmly as he could, never taking his eyes off of the dark brown ones staring back at him.

"Do you speak English, and if you do, I expect an answer and tell me why you were trespassing in my greenhouse young lady, and I expect an answer NOW!"

"It's not your greenhouse," she nearly shouted back, matching her pitch and intonation to his.

Surprised to hear her finally speak, and speak with such bravery, he genuinely smiled and chuckled. "So you can speak after all."

"Of course I can speak mister," she said, slowly growing her bravado. "And it's not your greenhouse," she added smugly.

"Oh is that so," he challenged, actually getting a kick out of the fearless kid standing defiantly in front of him. "Then whose is it? I live in that house and it's on my property young lady. And what is your name anyways and where do you live in town?"

Before she could answer any of his numerous questions, not that she was actually going to answer him anyway. She quickly turned her head and smiled, breaking her stare down with the tall man as she saw a four legged bundle of fur barreling towards them at full speed. She should have been scared seeing a full grown shepherd coming at her the way he was but she was in awe of his speed and beauty. He was far ahead of the lady that he had gone on the run with. He got within striking distance when Aedan shouted "Neiko heel," and the dog slid to a screeching halt at his side. His eyes were locked in on the young stranger but he heeded Aedan's command and didn't move from his position. Not paying any attention to Aedan's authority, the girl put her hand out and walked right up to the large Shepherd without hesitation. Neiko sniffed and lifted his left paw in welcome, and Nicole came jogging up to the threesome.

"Well hello, and who do we have here Aedan? You've made friends with this beautiful young lady and I wasn't even included?" she teased as she extended her hand out to the child staring back at her.

"Hi, I'm Nicole. And this here," she nodded towards her dog, "Is Neiko. Don't let his size scare you, he's a big baby and loves pretty ladies like yourself," Nicole said reassuringly, sizing up the girl, guessing she couldn't be more than 10 or 11.

"You can pet him if you'd like. He won't hurt you," she said reassuringly. She waited until the child finally gently started petting a now very docile Neiko. Once she touched his fur, she noticeably relaxed and crouched down and started petting him with both hands. While she was momentarily distracted, Nicole casually asked, "You now know our names. What should we call you?"

The girl never broke eye contact from the dog that was the center of her attention. "My name is Rainbow Elizabeth but all my friends call me Rainie."

"Well now Rainbow Elizabeth, or shall I say Rainie. It's very nice to meet you. Do you live close to here?"

Seeming to snap out of the trance that petting the dog had put her in, she almost sprung straight up and took a step toward the exit of the greenhouse.

"I've got to go," she announced, with an edge of panic in her voice.

Sensing that she was about to bolt, Nicole quickly glanced at Aedan and tried to think of a way to stop her. Before she could respond, Neiko came to the rescue by rolling over, begging for his belly to be rubbed. His soft whimpering caught the frightened girl's attention that tore between running away and going to her new friend's furry side. Neiko's eyes were what finally won her over. She knelt back down and started to slowly rub his belly which was greeted with the 100-pound shepherd practically purring at her touch.

Not quite sure what to say to keep the child from bolting, Nicole quickly said, "Rainie, you can stay as long as you want but I'm thirsty and am going inside for a cold soda. Would you like one before you head home?"

"My daddy doesn't let us drink much soda pop but I would really like one if that's okay."

"Sure, I have orange, mountain dew, or cola. Do you have a preference?"

"Orange please. Unless you have root beer, because that's my favorite."

"No, I'm sorry. We don't, but I promise to have some the next time you come to visit okay? Do you help out here in the greenhouse Rainie? There sure are some amazing plants in here," Nicole added as she ran inside their log cabin to grab the sodas. Rainbow continued to pet the dog, occasionally looking up at Aedan but saying nothing. Neither knew how to take the other, and both were too obstinate to give the other a break. When Nicole returned with their Orange Sodas just a moment later, Rainie nearly snatched it from her hand, but was polite and thanked her as she pulled the tab and started gosling it down. When she had emptied half the can, she looked up at the two of them standing side by side in some form of subconscious alliance and smiled.

"I've really got to go home now. Thanks, for the soda." And as she quickly exited the greenhouse and started off toward the woods, she shouted back.

"Yes, I do help in the greenhouse with my mother and the pretty blonde lady next door."

And with that she disappeared into the forest as the sun light waned.

Seeing her running into the already half darkened forest, Nicole become alarmed and yelled to the child but her question went unanswered as Rainbow Elizabeth Black had already disappeared into the night.

Chapter 18

Knowing that she had stayed away from home much longer than she should have, Rainie ran through the darkness as fast as her feet would take her. She knew the woods inside and out and even with the encroaching darkness, she sprinted towards her destination. She would have to think of an excuse for her absence and feared what the ramifications would be if her father figured out where she had ventured off to without supervision and without permission. She prayed that she could get to her mother for alliance before her father saw her. She continued to sprint, never slowing until she finally reached the river. Afraid of slipping on the wet river rock, she finally slowed her pace as she waded into the icy water and headed toward her home.

Chapter 19

Unsure what their visitor had wanted, or who she was or where she came from, Aedan and Nicole left the greenhouse and made their way back toward their tiny cabin with Neiko falling in behind them. They were greeted by an energetic pup as soon as they entered the cabin. Nicole hadn't allowed Sinjin to join them earlier when she'd run in for sodas, for fear that his ill-gotten behavior might intimidate or scare their young visitor. But after seeing her run into the woods and disappear into the night, she realized that it would take more than a rambunctious puppy to scare the likes of Rainbow Elizabeth. Thinking back to her first impression of the child, and how she looked nervous and slight terrified; Nicole realized now that she couldn't have been more wrong about the young lady. She wasn't nervous, she'd been indifferent to their interrogation and uninterested in answering their numerous questions. Her standoffish behavior made Nicole even more interested in learning more about her. But for now, the unanswered questions would have to wait as she had dishes to do.

Unable to get her many unanswered questions out of her head, she quickly called Danielle and invited them over for dessert and drinks; to which they gladly accepted. Nicole knew that Danny had lived in the tiny town long enough to know practically everyone in it, while Bruce was a lifelong resident of Mystique. Between the two of them, they'd be able to answer the questions swirling in her head as she quickly whipped up an angel food cake while Aaron Lewis serenaded she, and the dogs at her feet. She didn't even realize that she was swaying to the hypnotic rhythm emitting from her IPOD until Aedan came up behind her, and pulled her into his arms and twirled her around and into a slow dance in the middle of their cramped kitchen. They didn't talk, just let the rhythm of the song move their bodies as one. And for one brief second, she thought back to how many times she and Jared had done the same exact thing on their veranda overlooking the lake. Her heart still ached for him and somehow she knew that he would always be with her, but she also knew that he would have wanted her to be happy and for her to keep on living. So for the moment, she'd be content being held in the strong arms of the soldier who loved her, and who'd saved her life, in more ways than one.

Chapter 20

Danielle and Bruce barely made it inside the cabin before Nicole barraged them with questions. She started with asking about some of the visitors to the clinic, telling how many of them had come baring gifts, and offering them livestock, fruits, vegetables and eggs in exchange for medical treatment. Nicole laughed when Danielle and Bruce didn't seem surprised by her exclamation. Being a native of the area, Bruce tried to explain that the folks in Mystique didn't really place a high value on currency, and that many of them might not have vast wealth deposited in the one local bank in town, but they all paid whatever bills they owed, whether they bartered with the merchant or used cash. Bruce reassured both Nicole and Aedan, that no one in town would expect to have the service rendered at the clinic free of charge, and if they were paid in an unconventional way, he'd gladly exchange what they were given for cash. Having always worked in a large city hospital, the concept was completely foreign to Nicole, but even she had to admit that it had some merits, as she opened her refrigerator to get out some beer and revealed shelves full of produce.

Realizing that she was more fatigued that she'd realized, Nicole cornered Danielle when they were away from the guys and cut to the chase.

"Danielle, I have to ask you; we had a young girl visit us this evening. She couldn't have been more than 10 or 11 and Aedan found her wandering around alone in the greenhouse out back. From what I could tell, she appeared to be part Native American if that helps at all. Any idea who she is?"

Danielle remained silent for a brief moment, then responded.

"You say, you found her in the greenhouse, but she was alone?"

"Yes. Unless someone else was inside hiding, but I doubt there was anyone else with her. Aedan or Neiko would have known, so I would say that yes she was alone. Why?"

"Rainie's not allowed to cross the river without her mother. How long ago was this?" Danielle asked, with a hint of concern in her voice.

"She took off into the woods probably about an hour ago. And what do you mean cross the river?" Nicole asked, with obvious concern.

"Are you telling me that when that little girl took off into the woods, she had to cross that river to get home? She can't do that alone! Oh My God, that's too dangerous!" Nicole all but shrieked, racing to the window and looking out at the water, not sure what she expected to see.

Looking out at the darkened sky and unable to see across the river, Danielle shrugged.

"Too late to worry about it now Nic. There's nothing you can do. I just hope her father doesn't find out that she was over here. Make sure that neither you nor Aedan let it slip that she was here, when you meet her mother. Her mother and a few of the others venture out of their village, usually on the weekends, to help us with the plants."

Feeling slightly panicked, Nicole squared up to Danielle and asked earnestly, "Why can't we call her since you obviously know the family? I just want to make sure that she made it home alright. I had no idea that she was intending on crossing that river," Nicole exclaimed, feeling somewhat sick at the thought of what could have happened to the child.

"She made it back home Nicole. And they don't have phones in their community."

"What? How could they not have phones?"

"There wouldn't be coverage where they live, nor would they want it, even if there was coverage. Their village is across the river and very deep in the woods, at the base of Mystique Mountain. They are a very tight knit community and they don't welcome outsiders. So Nicole, don't you dare even think about venturing over there.

116

Do you understand me? I'm very serious Nic, stay away from their village. We are not welcome there."

Somewhat incensed and a little confused, she couldn't understand why Danielle was so adamant that she couldn't go to Rainbow's town but she dropped the subject as Aedan and Bruce joined them.

"Hey honey," Bruce said as came to Danielle's side, taking her into his arms. "Why don't we head back home and let these two relax a little."

Looking over at her brother and seeing the fatigue in his face reminded her of how pale and frail he had looked when he returned from the dessert. "You're tired Aedan, go to bed and we'll chat tomorrow night okay love," she said leaning into give her brother a peck on the cheek.

Realizing that she was right as usual, he didn't argue. Bruce and Danielle said their good byes and exited the cabin within two minutes. Once they were gone, Nicole told Aedan about her conversation with his sister about their guest. He too, felt concerned about the young girl departing the way she did but also had to agree with his twin, there was nothing that they could do about it. He quickly helped with the dishes and after letting the dogs out, he joined her in their bedroom.

They crawled into their bed and both were asleep within two minutes flat.

Chapter 21

"Where have you been child?" he all but demanded.

"I," she stammered, fidgeting with her hair, "I went for a walk father and I forgot the time. I'm sorry," she added for good measure.

"Did you cross the river and go into their town? Is that how you got that cut on your leg girl?"

Crossing her fingers behind her back, she defiantly looked her elderly father in the eyes and replied, "You know I wouldn't go into their town without mother." Hating that she was not telling the exact truth and twisting her response to satisfy her already fuming father, she prayed that her look of innocence was convincing enough to appease the irate man.

"And it's such a little cut father. I don't even remember getting it," she said looking down at the dried blood that had run down her shin.

"You have our community and do not need to mingle with those across the river child. You stay here with us and forget about them. Head my warning, and stay away from Mystique."

"But," she started to argue but was immediately cut off by the stern look that her father, her communities leader, was giving her and in that look, she knew that she couldn't push her luck any further and that any arguing was futile.

Chapter 22

Nicole and Aedan completed their first week running the clinic without any major glitches. They treated sprained ankles, taught crutch training, treated a few cases of poison ivy, one dog bite, a few injuries requiring stitches, one very poor child with the worst case of diaper rash that Nicole had ever seen, a couple cases of bronchitis and rounded out the week with a small outburst of some type of stomach bug. Many of the locals attributed it to their Chili contest that they'd all participated in at Earl Flemming's house while his wife was out of town visiting her sister. Aedan wasn't so certain that it was the chili, that sickened the men, but he treated their tore up insides just the same.

As promised, Danielle gave them space and time to ease into their new living arrangements and routine. She waited until Friday afternoon before she left a message on Aedan's cell, inviting them to go out with them later that evening, to which they accepted even though they were exhausted from their work week. Not quite sure what to expect, Nicole dressed conservatively in a pair of jeans, brown cowboy boots with black inlay and a black V-neck sweater which she accented with a tortoise and silver necklace and earrings. She touched up her make-up in the bathroom while Aedan was getting ready in their bedroom and when she finished, he was waiting for her in the living room. And he looked handsome, very, very handsome she thought to herself.

He looked up and she took his breath away.

"Hi, you look amazing Nicole. Absolutely amazing. You ready to go out and have a little fun?"

She smiled back at the man now standing in front of her. She was still uncomfortable with being the center of someone's attention, and felt herself blush as she turned away to grab her jean jacket and take a deep breath. With her back still toward him, she casually stated, "You don't look so bad yourself Aedan." Once her heart stopped racing, she turned back to face him.

"Ready when you are," she announced.

"And you do realize that this constitutes our first real date Aedan," she purred softly with a sparkle in her eyes, even though she truly was just teasing.

Pulling his arm out from behind his back, he displayed a handful of flowers that he'd obviously picked from the field by the cabin but none-the-less, they were beautiful.

"Well then I guess I'm glad I remembered to bring you flowers for our first date!" His smile said it all. And if she hadn't already, she would have fallen in love with him right and there.

"You brought me flowers?" she asked, feeling her heart doing pitter patters. "That was so sweet Aedan, thank you. But what made you think to pick flowers for me?"

"Damn woman, you were taking long enough in there getting ready, so I had time to kill. I let the dogs out one last time, and picked you some daisies. Not a big deal."

Walking up to him, she wrapped her arms around him and pulled him into a warm embrace. When she finally released him after nearly kissing the life right out of him, she smiled at the now silent man. "And yes, it is a big deal Aedan."

"God the woman could kiss," he thought to himself and knew that if they didn't leave to go out on the town immediately, they'd never make it out the door.

"Save some of that for when we get back Nic; please save some of that," he joked as he tapped her on the butt and opened the door for her.

They met Danielle and Bruce at a pub in the heart of town. Walking in, they were greeted by a few familiar faces, and warm smiles from those who recognized them. They were sized up by the locals that didn't and viewed them as newcomers. It wasn't until they made their way to the table where his sister was sitting, that he felt himself relax. He knew all too well how quickly small town rednecks fueled with alcohol could become unpredictable and that was a situation that he did not want to have to deal with. Sitting facing the exit, with his back to the wall, Aedan had a clear view of the bar and its' patrons. Once a soldier, always a soldier. Some habits die hard and he needed to be aware of his surroundings if he wanted to relax and enjoy the evening.

The evening flew by and before anyone knew it, it was almost one. Between the music, the dancing and the drinking, everyone had completely lost track of time. It had truly been their first date and even though Nicole did not consider them a couple, no one would have thought differently by the way Aedan held her in his arms as they danced to every slow country song. Even Danielle whispered to Bruce while they were taking a spin around the dance floor how happy she was to see her brother so content. Feeling the effects of the alcohol, Nicole didn't argue when Aedan stated that he'd drive her truck home at the end of the night. Just before leaving, Danielle reminded them both that typical Saturday mornings were spent in the greenhouse and garden, harvesting what was ready to be picked and that she'd be over by 8am. Nicole's head nearly split at the sounds of her anticipated arrival time but agreed half-heartedly stating that she'd see them then.

Once home, they took care of the dogs, washed up and climbed into bed together. Ever the gentleman,

Aedan had already decided that as much as he wanted her, it wouldn't be fair of him to take advantage of the fact that Nicole had drank significantly more than he had during the course of the evening and when they made love again, he definitely wanted her to remember it. Of course, that thought went right out the window when she rolled over and pulled him to her.

Chapter 23

Morning came early when her two dogs heard Danielle's roster next door announce that the sun was rising. Neiko and Sinjin, though not in the bedroom she now shared with Aedan, made it very clear with their incessant barking that they were awake and ready to play. When she finally began to stir, knowing that she couldn't ignore them any longer, she was momentarily afraid to lift her head as she quickly remembered just how much she had consumed the night before. Slowly she rolled over and was face to face with a smiling man who was propped up on his elbow and grinning ear to ear.

"Well good morning gorgeous. How's the head this morning?"

"Hi." Even with her alligator breath, she leaned in and gave him a quick kiss. "Mine's fine, how's yours," she asked, smiling back at him with a wicked, come and get me look in her eyes. Wanting to go another round like the one they'd had just hours before, he pulled her close and kissed her longingly. "I'm fine," he responded when they finally parted lips.

"That you are Aedan." As the same thought process formulated inside her head, she heard Neiko's bark change and knew that it was time to get up and any fun would have to wait until later. Taking her cue, Aedan pulled back the covers and got out of bed. Nicole momentarily enjoyed the view before getting out of bed herself and getting old clothes on. Having no way of knowing what time to expect the gardeners to show up, she pulled her hair into a ponytail after washing up in the bathroom. She opened the door to the aroma of Aedan's coffee brewing and was greeted by two energetic dogs at her feet. Crouching down to give them both her attention, she looked over at Aedan who was pouring milk in the cup of tea that he'd already made for her. Looking at her surroundings and the path her life was currently following, Nicole for the first time in a long time felt truly blessed and content. She was surrounded by things that made her happy and was finally, once again, working in the one profession she was meant to do. She was a nurse through and through and even though working in the clinic might not be as structured and fulfilling as the trauma nursing she'd done back in Syracuse, these patients needed her just as much. She might have only one week of experience under her belt working in the clinic, but already Nicole felt that this is where she was meant to be.

Sipping on her cup of tea, and whipping up a quick omelet with some of the vegetables they'd been given throughout the week. Nicole chuckled when she realized that every ingredient that they were consuming for their breakfast, with the exception or her tea and Aedan's coffee, had come from the land around her. The cheese and milk came from Mrs. Jones' goats, the eggs were compliments of Danielle's chickens, the ham was from an elderly farmer who came in with a lame hip, and the vegetables had been donated by several of the patrons who had stopped by the clinic simply to introduce themselves. Even the bread had been fresh baked by one of the women from the church group who stopped in to visit before they'd closed up for the week.

"Hey," she said, to get Aedan's attention. "Do you realize that I believe we're officially homesteaders of some type," she chuckled. "Not one thing from our breakfast meal came prepackaged or from a store. Maybe these folks up here are on to something. I mean, I love the concept of not having to spend tons of money on food that's shipped in from overseas or filled with a bunch of preservatives, you know."

"There's nothing wrong with living off the land and being self-sufficient Nic. Why do you think so many of the people in this town have solar, hydropower, wood fueled furnaces and massive gardens, along with various livestock and poultry?"

"I thought it was just because it's a rural little town in the mountains and that's what country people do," she responded sincerely. "I mean, I was raised in the country as well, but we didn't go to this extreme by any means.

I'm not mocking or judging them Aedan. I'm actually quite envious of their knowledge and ability to be so self-reliant and maybe once I get to know some of the women, they'll be able to educate me a little and give me some helpful hints." Glancing out the window, she smiled.

"Oh look, here comes Danny now with some of them."

Nicole and Aedan went outside to greet them, leaving their dogs inside for fear that their size and breed might intimidate the women. Before they even got to the women, Danielle was the first to speak.

"Where are the pups? Not one of these ladies is afraid of a couple of dogs Aedan, so you might as well let them out so they can meet my friends. After all, Neiko and Sinjin need to be familiar with them. They'll be plenty of times that they come over here when you might not be around."

Looking over at Nicole who nodded her approval, Aedan opened the front door for the dogs to make their escape outside. The women standing beside Aedan's sister were virtually unfazed by the flurry of fur as Nicole's two dogs raced out and around them. They sniffed, barked and raced around the women trying to gain their attention. It only took a few minutes for the dogs to settle down and get used to have the additional people. After Danielle had finished the introductions with Nicole trying to memorize the women's names, she found herself slightly disappointed that Rainie's mother was not amongst the group. She didn't want to betray the young girls' confidences but she remained very curious about her. The women, along with Aedan worked together caring for the plants, harvesting the grown produce, watering, providing nutrients, thinning the plants where necessary, and planting new seeds for a mid-winter harvest. When Aedan asked how they expected to grow plants in the middle of the winter in northern New Hampshire, he was quickly shut down by more than one in the group. Nicole simply chuckled to herself when he tried to overanalyze how the greenhouse worked so well, despite the climate. She waited until she and Danielle were out of earshot of the other women to broach the subject with Aedan's sister.

"Great turnout today Danielle. The ladies seem so knowledgeable about all aspects of gardening. I really had no idea how much work was involved in having a successful garden. Are these the usual group of ladies who come to help routinely?" she asked nonchalantly.

Having no idea that she was fishing for information, Danielle answered honestly. "There are a few others who routinely come but they don't have phone service where they live so we never know exactly when they'll show up," she said as she gently thinned the cherry tomato plants in her hands. Looking up, she smiled. "Speak of the devil, here they are now."

Nicole looked up and into the eyes of two very leery women who were very quickly sizing her up. Nicole knew immediately that at least one of the women was related to Rainie but she never let on and allowed them to inspect her while she remained silent for just a brief second before extending her hand in welcome.

"Hello. What you women are doing here, is nothing short of amazing," she exclaimed, seeing the tension radiating from the women immediately gone.

"I have never seen such a massive assortment of fruits and vegetables all grown not only in one place but inside a greenhouse. What you've done here has put any garden I've ever had completely to shame."

The older women spoke first.

"Thank you. Our family and our ancestors have lived off the land and what is provided to us by mother earth for as long as I can remember. If you are willing to help us, we can teach you some of our secrets as well."

"That would be really great. Do you ladies live in town and come over frequently? Aedan and I both work at the clinic all day Monday through Friday so if you ever come in the evening, or anytime on the weekends, you'll find me here and yes, I would love to learn through you women how to grow plants like this," she said as gestured to the plants in front of her. Is it just the two of you that come to help Danielle out?" she asked, hoping that Rainie's name would be mentioned.

Somewhat leery of a stranger, the older woman again spoke first.

"No, there are others. But usually it's Star and I who come over. And," she said while extending her hand, "We haven't been properly introduced. I am Moriah. And you are?" she asked.

Knowing that she was being scrutinized, Nicole willed herself to not be intimidated by the weathered but dignified looking woman standing in front of her. She and the woman who called herself Moriah were the same height and both had green eyes that seemed to pierce into the other's soul but neither appeared afraid. Nicole took the elderly woman's hand and immediately felt a jolt of electricity go through her body but didn't flinch. Quickly regaining her composure, she smiled and glanced over at the younger woman and then back at Moriah.

"My name is Nicole Brentwood, and the guy half covered in potting soil over there," she said, gesturing over at Aedan, "Aedan is Danielle's twin brother, and my roommate. It's very nice meeting you both."

Star quickly stepped forward and reached to shake her hand as well. Nicole again felt a jolt of electricity, though this time not nearly the intensity of Moriah's. Going on her gut, she again smiled at the women.

"You two are related. If my hunch is correct, are you mother and daughter? Though you Moriah, hardly look old enough to be Star's mother," she added for good measure.

"You are very observant Nicole," Moriah responded. "And yes, Rainie is my granddaughter," she added.

Seeing one quick second of recognition flicker on Nicole's face was all she needed to see to know that her intuition had been correct and that Rainie had in fact crossed the river without their knowledge. Nicole didn't fall for the bait and didn't respond or question her statement and luckily for all, Danielle spoke next.

"Moriah, where is my little friend Rainie? I haven't seen her around in a while."

Star spoke up first. "She wasn't feeling too well this morning so we let her sleep in. Maybe she'll come with us next week Danny," she meekly responded.

Feigning only mild interest, Nicole asked the younger woman what was wrong with her daughter. Star's simple reply was that the child had come down with a fever and just needed to rest to sleep it off and that she'd been given an herbal tea that was sure to break the fever. Nicole didn't think anything of it as she knew children could get low grad temps for numerous reasons, and with that, the women joined the rest of the group who were already hard at work.

The group worked for the most part silently for the first hour, each working on a specific area or task that had been assigned to them. Nicole was working alongside Danielle, while one of the women from the village had Aedan thinning starter plants. Lost in her own little world, she hadn't even realized that she'd started humming at first, then softly singing to herself. It wasn't until Danielle joined in, and slowly, one by one the women inside of the massive greenhouse joined in. Though the song wasn't familiar to neither Moriah nor Star, they quickly picked up on the lyrics and joined in on the chorus. Soon the volume of their voices was turned up and the Eagles' Hotel California could probably be heard all the way back to Mystique. Aedan excused himself after a half hour or so, so that he could check on Nicole's dogs and also give the women their space. They stayed within the confines of the greenhouse for another hour and then, as quickly as they had appeared to help, they disappeared just as quickly; going off in various directions. Danielle walked into the cabin that Aedan was sharing with Nicole without knocking and made herself at home in their refrigerator, grabbing a beer for both she and Nicole as Aedan rejoined them, making his way to Nicole's side. Neiko and Sinjin were in front of him, racing toward her, showing their excitement by jumping and barking in delight as she crouched down to meet their kisses. Standing, she was handed a beer and greeted by a quick kiss from Aedan as he put his arm around her waist and pulled her close, a move that didn't go unnoticed by Danielle.

"Wow that was fun!" Nicole said in between swallows of her ice cold beer.

"What's the scoop on Star and Moriah? They definitely are unique, so to speak" Nicole asked.

"They are good people. They just prefer to keep to themselves and stay close to their community. They come across the river to join us here at the greenhouse because of their love of gardening, not because they need the food we're growing here. They have three greenhouses twice as big as this one back in their village. Give them time to get to know you a little more Nicole and once they trust you, they'll open up more and you'll be shocked when you realize just how intelligent they are. Moriah is a wealth of knowledge on many topics and there isn't anything that she can't fix, cure or heal utilizing the herbs and plants that she grows. In olden days, she would have been referred to as a medicine woman but that term is quite archaic don't you think," she asked in between gulps of beer.

"Now days, she's just referred to as an elder."

"Are they Native Americans or what type of community do they live in Danielle? And I don't remember seeing any bridges going over the river so other than crossing on foot, so how do you get to their town?" Nicole asked, now intrigued.

"You don't. They cross the river downstream where it's shallowest to come over to Mystique. They hardly ever go into town, they usually just come here or occasionally over to Sally's. And the closest bridge crossing over to their side of the river is about five miles east of here and from what I'm told, the road leading into their village is unmarked and very similar to the ones you had heading into the Lodge that you guys stayed in in Maine."

"You're not making any sense Danielle," Nicole asked, somewhat confused. "What are you talking about? You've never been to their home? And you make it sound like they don't want anyone to know how to get to their town."

"Nope, didn't say that. I'm just saying that they are a community that prefers to remain isolated from the outside world. From what Star has told me, they are very self-contained and have everything we have here in

Mystique and therefore they don't need to leave their village often. Star said that a few of the men work outside of their community but for the most part, they are farmers or trappers. The children are homeschooled until age 16, and then they're kicked out of the village, much like the Amish, and thrown into the outside world to fend for themselves."

"That is awful," Nicole said, shocked. "How is a 16 year old expected to survive on his or her own in a world that they've been isolated from all their lives?"

"Precisely," Danielle responded. "They're given one month on their own to see if they want to live outside their community. If yes, then they're on their own. If not, then they're welcome to return to their village and take their place in the community as an adult. From what I'm told, their town is quite large and though most of the people in it were born and raised there, there are some outsiders who have joined them by marrying someone from within the community so in that aspect, they differ from the Amish."

"What do they live in? You make it sound like they're a bunch of Indians or Nomads or a Commune or something."

"I assume they live in homes, like ours."

"What do you mean you assume? Haven't you ever been to their homes Danielle?"

"Nope," Danielle responded. "No reason for me to go over there, and I've never been invited," she responded honestly.

Looking at Aedan's sister in disbelief, you mean to tell me you've lived here for how many years and have these women coming over to your property to spend time with you but you've never asked to visit them in their village? Haven't you at least been curious?" she asked.

"Sure I've been curious Nicki. But you don't go where you're not invited. And I hope that you remember that while you're living up here. Country people will help you with anything you need and will always be there for you. But most of us live in this rural, isolated area for a reason. And out here, we respect each other's privacy and keep to ourselves."

"Point taken."

"Not trying to be rude, bossy or pushy, it's just that's the way it is in the North Country. In the city I believe the saying is fences make good neighbors. Well around here, it's the same thing only we're not separated by fences but by acreage. Everyone minds their own business and that's the way it's always been and the way we like it."

"I get it Danielle, I really do; but aren't you at least a little bit curious about how and where Star and Moriah live?"

It was Aedan who finally stepped in and ended the conversation, knowing by his sister's facial expression that she didn't want to discuss the matter anymore.

"Danny, you hungry?" he asked. It's well past lunch time and I was about to throw a couple of burgers on the grill for Nic and I. Would you like one?

"Nah, thanks love. Bruce must be wondering where I am by now so I'll scoot on home. And Aedan and Nicole," she said as she headed toward the door, "You both did really well today. You were a lot of help and the women all thought you were as cute as can be," she said, winking at her brother as she made her escape, closing the door behind her.

Before Nicole could say a word, Aedan grabbed her and pulled her into an embrace, which nearly took her breath away as their chests collided. Then he pulled her lips to his and did take her breath away with a kiss that lasted just long enough to get her attention and that of every nerve cell in her body. When they finally parted lips, she eventually managed to regain her senses.

"And what exactly was that kiss for?"

"That Nicole, was because you are amazing. And," he said, patting her on her rump as he picked up the burgers and started to head outside to the grill, "because I've wanted to do that for the last two hours. Now go take a quick shower while I'm grilling these burgers. I've already showered and I think I probably left you a little bit of hot water," he said grinning.

"After that kiss Aedan, it's okay if the water's cold," she said as she headed toward the bathroom, dogs in tow.

Chapter 24

The remainder of the weekend flew by and before they knew it, it was Monday morning and time for another week at the clinic. Nicole was not nearly as nervous to start the work week as she had been previously. The staff was in the kitchenette when they arrived and greeted them warmly. After yet another cup of coffee, Aedan was ready to tackle the crowd forming in the waiting room.

The day was filled with a few sprains, a few lacerations, several cases of bronchitis and even more cases of what Nicole referred to as fall crud. Aedan prescribed a few inhalers, a few antibiotics and a lot of chicken soup. Everyone left satisfied with the care that they had received. Just as the afternoon started winding down, Meghan hesitantly approached Nicole and then Aedan. Before she could even get the words out, Nicole looked up to see Danielle and Star in the doorway. Surprised by their appearance, Aedan knew something was immediately wrong when he looked at their ashen faces.

"We need you both to come with us now," Danielle said, and then turned to exit the clinic.

"Where Danny," Aedan said as he followed the two women outside. "What's wrong Danny? I need to know where we're going before I go anywhere!" he demanded.

It was Star who spoke, and her words chilled Nicole to the bone.

"It's my daughter, we can't break her fever, and now she won't wake up and I think she's dying."

Nicole and Aedan exchanged looks. Nicole nodded as if knowing what he was thinking and quickly went into the back office, reappearing within thirty seconds with a bag over her shoulder.

"Take us to her Star," was all she said as they rushed out the door following the women. Nicole turned back quickly and yelled to Meghan to take care of her dogs for her. "The door is unlocked," is the last thing she heard as the four exited the clinic and raced off to try and save the child's life.

"Come on, Bruce has the horses waiting. Nicole, I hope you know how to ride well because it's going to be a rough ride," she added.

Rushing them out the door, leaving the staff at the clinic behind, Nicole simply said, "I can ride, and won't hold you up, so let's go!"

The four of them jumped into Danielle's waiting truck and raced towards her home where Bruce had their three horses ready and waiting.   Star and Danielle shared one horse, while Nicole and Aedan each jumped on their own rides. Before they took off, Bruce assured them that he'd bring the truck around to their village via the county route that lead into their community in case the child required more care than they could provide her within the confines of her home. Before Star could argue, he assured her that he'd deal with the consequences. He smiled warmly, and barreled out of their driveway and down the road.

Nicole threw the bag of supplies from the clinic into her back pack and cinched it tightly around her waist. Seeing that she was ready to ride, Danielle took off down the embankment and led her horse down to the water's edge. Wasting no time, they all entered the frigid water and crossed without incident and once out of the current, took off at a near gallop. As they raced towards her village, Star worried about how her daughter who had appeared to be getting better yesterday, but by this morning, looked gravely ill; but also worried about how her family and community would react to her bringing the outsiders into the sanctity of their environment. But at the moment she didn't care. She thought only of her daughter and how she looked when she had left to seek help. Nothing that they had done to break the fever had worked and out of desperation, Star had made the decision to go against her husband and mother, and seek outside help. Now she was bringing two virtual strangers and her only true friend from outside their community into her home; all the while praying that their medicine would be enough to save her daughter's life. She led the way along the well-worn trail into the dense forest and within three minutes via horseback, was entering their tiny grouping of homes. As neighbors looked on silently, she dismounted her ride and motioned for them to join her as she walked briskly toward her home. Star opened the door as wide as its worn hinges would stretch and motioned them in. The three followed her inside and were stuck immediately by the strong aroma of vinegar and garlic. Being an excellent cook, Nicole couldn't think of what they could possibly been cooking that consisted of garlic and vinegar together. They made their way into a darkened room and once Aedan gazed down at the child, he felt a chill go down his spine. Nicole, on the other hand, felt pain at seeing the acutely ill child lying still as death. The elderly woman that she had come to know as Moriah looked up at the invasion into her home and then at her daughter who stood behind the three silently.

"Star, what have you done? We take care of our own!" she nearly shouted.

"Mother, you are a wonderful healer, and have cured all of us of many ailments ever since I was Rainie's age. But Momma, she is my child and she is dying and we need more medicine than what you can provide. Let the doctor save my baby, please!"

Reluctantly, Moriah nodded and immediately both Aedan and Nicole were at the child's side while Moriah continued to rub the child's head with a cloth wet with vinegar trying to pull out the fever.

"We take care of our own here," she continued to whisper, as she frantically rubbed the child's head.

Knowing how hard it must be for the elderly woman to admit that her knowledge of homeopathic medicine wasn't enough to cure her own granddaughter, Aedan looked into her weathered face and into eyes that held many secrets.

"Moriah, is it alright if I call you Moriah mam," he asked out of a sign of respect for the obvious matriarch of the family. Again, she nodded ever so slightly as he noted tears starting to well up in her eyes as she looked down at the child whose head was still nestled in her lap.

"You've done a fine job here. The garlic has been essential for helping keep this child's fever from getting any hotter, and the vinegar helps pull it away from her. If they're not working as well as we both know they should, then we have to find the underlying cause of her fever and take care of it so her body can heal itself. How long has she been ill?" he asked, shifting his glance between the two women. Before either of them could respond, Star's irate husband stormed into the home looking like he was ready for war. Star tried to cut him off at the door, but was pushed aside as the made his way to the man crouched at his daughter's side.

"What is the meaning of this? You are not welcome here!"

Aedan immediately stood up ready to confront the irate man standing shoulder to shoulder to him. If attacked, he wanted to be vertical and prepared for any altercation that might occur. Nicole was between the two men in two seconds flat.

"You must be Rainie's father," she said, not giving the angry man even time to think about an answer. She reached up, shaking the man's hand, even though it hadn't been offered to her.

"We respect your village and your hesitancy to have anyone who doesn't live here invade your home. But sir, I don't have any children yet and someday when I do, I would give anything to have him or her be like your daughter. So please let me try and help her. Moriah," she said, glancing up at the weathered, tired face of his mother-in-law, "has taken very good care of your daughter, but sometimes, our mother earth doesn't provide the raw essentials that we need to heal everything. So in those instances, we need to take what she has provided us and mix it with man-made ingredients to create medicine that is stronger, not necessarily better. And I would be honored if you would allow the Dr and I to help your daughter. We only want to help Moriah's medicine work well; please sir…"

Star's husband's face revealed nothing of what he was thinking. Aedan stood ready for an altercation while Nicole stared down the menacing looking man standing over her. Her posture never wavered as the man standing nearly six inches taller than she remained silent and rigid in posture. It took nearly ten seconds before saying nothing, he took a step back, allowing Nicole and Aedan to return to his daughter's side. Nicole immediately took out a thermometer, and checked an axillary temp as the semi-conscious child couldn't hold it in her mouth. Hearing the beep indicating that the temperature had registered, Nicole looked up at Aedan and mouthed "101.8".

Knowing that an axillary temp was usually approximately one degree less than a true oral temp, both she and Aedan quickly realized how gravely ill the child was. Her heart was tacky and pulse thready, and Aedan noted how shallow her respirations were, despite using her accessory abdominal muscles. The child lying in front of him was probably septic; and his job was to figure out as quickly as possible what was poisoning her. He drilled both parents and her grandmother as subtlety as possible, while Nicole took her blood pressure and while protecting her privacy, evaluated the child's mouth, and torso for signs of injury. It wasn't until she pulled up the child's pajama leg that she gasped and caught everyone's attention. Everyone looked down at the source of her reaction; and Aedan knew immediately upon seeing the obviously infected raw festering wound on the child's shin that she was indeed septic. He didn't need to tell Nicole what to do. Before he even opened his mouth, she was pulling out supplies from her back pack to start an IV. Wanting to take the time to console Rainie's mother who was now crying after seeing her daughter's injury, Nicole whispered to Danielle to take her out to get some air while she started the intravenous. Star felt like she was going to pass out so she obliged and left the tiny room. When Danielle tried to convince her husband to leave also, he said nothing but the way he crossed his arms indicated that he wasn't going anywhere. She respected his wishes and guided an unsteady Star outside and away from the ciaos. Outside, Danielle was met by nearly a dozen neighbors who had converged on the tiny home. The men in attendance had seen to the horses, rubbing them down and feeding them; while the women folk were at Stars' side for strength and support.

Only the few that knew Danielle even acknowledged her presence and suddenly Danielle felt as if she'd stepped into the twilight zone. She knew that she was silently being scrutinized and didn't like the feeling of being an outsider who was in a place where she wasn't necessarily wanted. Just when she was starting to feel very uncomfortable, she heard the tell-tale sound of Bruce's truck. She'd know the sound of his noisy muffler anywhere and felt a sigh of relief when he came into view. Cutting the engine and stepping out, she only stared as he greeted the men in a language that she didn't understand, or even realize that he knew how to speak.

"Who was this man, her fiancée that she'd known for years; and how the hell did Bruce know whatever the language was that he was speaking," she thought to herself. But at the moment, she didn't care. She was just happy to have his alliance at her side. He continued talking in whatever language it was was as he made his way to her. As he put his arm around her, he gestured to the men and women in attendance and said her name. Everyone seemed to immediately dissolve their indifference to her, and now she had absolutely no idea what was going on.

"How's the child?" he asked, leaning in to kiss her cheek.

"She's very ill Bruce," she responded quietly. "How the hell do you know how to speak whatever the hell

148

language that was that you were speaking," she asked under her breath.

"It's a long story Danny; a tale for another time. But I explained to them that Aedan and Nicki are here to help and they appreciate it."

Inside, unaware of Bruce's presence, Nicole felt herself starting to sweat as she searched for a good vein to use to start her IV. As she searched, she quickly realized just how dehydrated the poor child was. Once she got a good blood return, she hung a liter bag of fluids while Aedan looked at what antibiotic options he had at his disposal, silently thanking Nicole for having the insight to grab not only oral, topical antibiotics and sterile water for irrigating the leg wound, but also for bringing a good assortment of broad spectrum IV antibiotics as well. Confirming that the child had no known allergies, but then again, she'd never taken any man made antibiotics before; Aedan chose the one that he felt would cover the large spectrum of organisms that could be causing the infection that the child was suffering from. As he hung it, while her skeptical father looked on, he silently prayed that they'd gotten to her in time. As he hung the antibiotic, her grandmother continued to stroke the sleeping child's head, repeatedly saying the same two lines over and over, in a language that was foreign to everyone in the room except for her son-in-law.

When the IV antibiotics were up and starting to infuse, Nicole gently washed out and irrigated the wound on Rainie's leg and it was only then that the child showed any form of movement. Knowing that it must be very painful for her, she tried to be as gentle as possible and as she continued to clean out the pus from the ragged edges of the wound, she quietly whispered a Gaelic song to the child, instilling Rainie's name into the verse. The tune told of a brave child who battled dragons to return to her family and somehow seemed appropriate for the battle that Rainbow was now facing. Moriah continued to hold the child's head, gently stroking her long black hair away from her face, and she continued to repeat over and over the same words, going into a near trance. Once finished cleaning the wound, Nicole gently applied a dressing and adjusted the child's clothing. None of her moves went unnoticed as her father watched over everyone with the eyes of a hawk. When she was done covering Rainie with a thin cotton sheet, she stood and quietly excused herself while Aedan sat beside the child, lost in thought.

Nicole exited the house to find a crowd had now congregated outside of Star's modest home. Some of the faces were familiar as they were women she'd met at the greenhouse just a few days prior. She also saw that Bruce had made it into the village with his old but faithful truck. She noted that he was not only talking to Star, but also to the many strangers that were present. As she made her way over toward Danielle, she saw Bruce wipe a lone tear from Star's face. Both she and Danielle saw the action and while both had reactions to the gesture, neither passed judgment.

"It'll be okay Star. Aedan will make sure that Rainie will be okay. She has a nasty infection in her leg and that's the cause of her fever. I promise you, we won't let anything happen to your daughter."

"Thank You Nicole," Bruce said sincerely. Taking both of Danielle's hands, he kissed them gently. "It's time you know the truth Danielle," he said sincerely. "All of the truth."

Not liking the sound of his words, but trusting her instincts and her man, Danielle's glaze never wavered from his. "Okay, tell me Bruce, tell me everything," she said, smiling up at the love of her life.

"Rainie is my niece, Star my sister, and Moriah is my mother. And this was my home growing up."

Hearing the words actually leave his lips was not only cathartic but liberating. Tradition made it forbidden to ever speak about his family since he'd chosen life outside the village. This had been the one and only secret that he'd ever kept from her and he had hated not telling Danielle the truth all these years. He hadn't directly lied when he'd told her years ago when they'd first met that he had no family left and was alone in the world. When, at age 16, he had decided that he wanted, actually needed, to live outside of their community; he had been shunned by everyone that he'd left behind. It wasn't until years later, and happenstance that he'd run into one of his former best friends from their tight knit community, and that friend had let it slip to Star that her only brother had come back to the area and was living essentially just across the river from her. Initially, without her husband knowing, Star risked everything by crossing the Mystique River, just to catch a glimpse of her brother. But as fate would have it, she met Danielle instead. Polar opposite in appearance and personality as they could possibly be, they struck up a conversation, and eventual friendship was formed. Granted, Star's ulterior motive was initially only to see her brother again, a fact that Danielle was just now discovering. Originally, she'd come for that reason alone. But Star had returned week after week because she'd come to care about Danielle as much as she would have if she too had been flesh and blood.

Danielle remained motionless and speechless, absorbing what she'd just been told. It was Star who spoke next.

"It's true Danny. We are, were siblings, she corrected. And Moriah is not only my mother, but Bruce's as well."

"You came from here? And all along, your family has been living just a few miles from us. Yet you never told me?" she asked, somewhat dumbfounded.

"He couldn't tell you Danielle. The day he left us, is the day he became an orphan," she simply replied.

"I knew you said that you didn't have any family," she said, with sudden complete clarity of what he'd said synapsing in her brain.

"Oh my God, you mean to tell me that you've really been alone, as in no one to help you out, since you were just 16 years old Bruce? Oh my God," she said, almost hyperventilating, "How did you survive alone at such a young age?"

"It's just what we did if we left the community Danielle. It's just the way it was, and still is. I left the same way that my aunt had years before. I figured since she never came back, the outside world couldn't be all that scary. I knew of a few others as well, and they never returned so neither did I."

"Well, excuse me for saying so; but that is ridiculous, stupid, a form of child abuse if you ask me, and inexcusable on any parent's part." Suddenly she had the attention of everyone within hearing range.

Nicole spoke up. "Danielle, that isn't the way the elders or community would see it. I know it might sound mean to you, but their society has rules, just like every other society. And Bruce knew what the rules were when he chose to leave. Societies only survive and work if the rules are followed, regardless of how harsh they sound to outsiders. I'm sorry, I have to agree with the elders; he chose to leave, so he was no longer welcome here."

Danielle didn't like what she was hearing, but was forced to agree with Nicole.

"Ah baby, I'm so sorry that you had to go through what you did. And you," she said, gesturing to her friend Star.

"Come over here and let me hug my future sister-in-law. Shunned or not, you still have the same blood running through you that the love of my life does, so that makes us family." Before Star could react, her husband appeared at the door and summoned his wife in their native tongue. She nearly jumped at his command and raced inside.

"What did he say?" Nicole asked the crowd, specifically Bruce.

"He said that Rainie moved her hand when asked a question, as if she understood."

"Oh my God, come one! Let's go check on her," she said, gesturing to Bruce and Danielle. The three of them raced into the tiny, sparsely lit room to find Aedan still at the child's side, and her grandmother still at her head, stroking her gently and speaking in whispers. She still looked as if she was in a trance and everyone remained silent, waiting for Aedan to speak. Aedan motioned for Star to take her daughter's hand, which she did.

Aedan spoke softly to the motionless child in front of him.

"Rainie honey, your momma and daddy are here with you now, and your Uncle Bruce and your future Auntie. We need you to let us know you can hear us baby. Can you squeeze your momma's hand if you can hear us and understand?" he asked gently. Not sure what would happen, the room went completely still. The child didn't wake up or speak, but Star nearly jumped up when she felt the light squeeze on her hand. She burst out sobbing feeling her daughter's touch.

"She moved! She squeezed my hand!" she exclaimed, barely able to contain her joy. "My baby can hear us and is getting better."

Trying not to squash the joy in the room, and wanting everyone to be realistic, Aedan spoke up.

"That's a good sign Star, a real good sign but she'd not out of the woods yet. It's going take more than one dose of antibiotics to clear up the infection that our girl has. It's now, what, nearly 4 o'clock in the afternoon, and she'll need another dose at midnight and again at 8 am so if it's alright with you both," he said glancing between Star and her husband, I will sleep here on the floor tonight so that I can give her two more doses before I have to be at the clinic tomorrow." Star and her husband exchanged looks but didn't get an opportunity to respond. It was Star's mother who made the decision for all of them.

"You will be our guest. And you will sleep not on the floor but in my home. I will make sure that you are back at my granddaughter's side in time enough to give her your medicine if you assure me that it will help my granddaughter."

"Moriah, I will do everything in my power to help your granddaughter recover. I promise you that."

Nicole spoke up. "It will cure your granddaughter Moriah, I give you my word. She will be awake and back to herself before you know it. And Moriah, you started the healing process with all that you did to keep her fever from going any higher. You are the reason that our medicine will be able to help her heal, and our medicine will break her fever and rid her body of the toxins in it but it will take time. Trust us and we will help your granddaughter heal. And it isn't necessary that we stay in your home, there is plenty of room for us to sleep right here beside Rainie should she need anything."

"You do not need to stay here Nicole. You should go back with Danielle so you can take care of the dogs."

"No," she cut him off, squaring her shoulders to him. "We will be staying here together to take care of her together. You stay, I stay. Your sister said she'd take care of the dogs. I intend to be here with you when our girl opens her eyes, and with a little luck, she will do that soon."

Moriah settled their argument.

"You will both stay, and you will both stay with me. It is settled. Star, show our guests to my home. There is nothing more they can do for the child right now and they need nourishment."

"With all due respect Moriah, I need to be here to monitor her throughout the night."

"No, I will be here until your medicine is due again, and I will summon you if I see a change. It's settled," she said, dismissing them.

Knowing there was no sense in arguing with the matriarch of the family, they nodded and in understanding, quietly exited the room. Once outside, Nicole spoke quietly with Danielle who was still reeling from the news that Bruce had told her. Danielle nodded and mounted her ride as she needed to get across the river before the sun set. Reassuring Bruce that she knew the way back, she took off toward home, happy for the solitude the ride would afford before she had to face him again. Although she and Aedan had been orphaned at a young age, her mind kept swirling around the fact that the most important person in the world to her, other than her brother, had been left to fend for himself since he was just a teenager, and that fact upset her beyond words. As she rode, she was so caught up in everything that was racing through her mind, that she wasn't aware that she was no longer alone on her journey home.

Chapter 25

Nicole slept in cat naps curled up beside Aedan until it was time for Rainie's next dose of antibiotics. She was gently awakened just prior to midnight and quickly pulled her hair up and out of her face. She found Moriah standing in the doorway watching her silently. Once at the child's side, she immediately noted that the child's respirations weren't nearly as labored as they had been earlier in the day. Star and her husband sat beside they child's bed, both lost in their own thoughts and both praying for their only daughter's recovery. Aedan checked her vital signs as Nicole hung the antibiotic and another bag of IV solution, now kicking herself for only bringing two bags with her as she had had no idea what they were walking into when they were first summoned across the river. Nicole starting talking to the child, chatting away as if they were once again in the greenhouse tending to their plants, not fighting for the child's life. Nicole kept talking away, rambling on about the plants, about her dogs, what her life was like in Maine and what her summers had been like growing up in New York. The child continued to sleep soundly, appearing oblivious to the conversation going on at her bedside, but that didn't matter to her; she kept on talking as if her captive audience was wide awake and answering her back. Nicole knew from experience that even patients in comas said that they'd heard the conversations going on around them when they were under so she assumed that her little patient could probably hear her in the same way. In between stories, Nicole whispered over and over in Rainie's ear that it was up to her to come back to them and how much she was needed here on this earth and that she would achieve big things someday. She just needed to decide to stay with them and let the medicine heal her body. As the antibiotic finished infusing, Nicole gently lifted her pajama leg to check the dressing placed earlier over the gaping wound on her shin. Noting that it hadn't bled through, she decided to leave it intact until the morning and let the child rest without additional pain. Once finished, she and Aedan wearily made their way back to Moriah's home and tried to get some sleep before morning arrived.

As the sun rose, so did Aedan. He silently slid away from Nicole as she slept, lost in a dream. As he stepped out into the tiny living room of the elderly woman's home, he was greeted by Moriah and a hot cup of coffee. Startled that he hadn't heard any movement since waking, but yet here she was, coffee in hand, smiling at her guest.

"Good morning Moriah," he whispered.

"Good morning Doctor," she replied back.

"Please just call me Aedan."

"Okay Aedan. Mind if I ask you something," she asked, all the while studying him.

"Shoot," he replied as he sipped on the steaming coffee, brewed to perfection.

"Do you have regrets?"

"Regrets? About what?"

"Do you have regrets about going to war," the matriarch asked, never deviating her eyes from his. "That's what cost you your leg correct?"

Surprised in her observation, he simply asked, "What makes you think I was in a war, and lost a leg?"

Moriah couldn't help but laugh.

"Do you take us for fools my friend? You walk like a soldier, talk like a soldier, and carry yourself with the self-assurance of a soldier. I am not concerned about how you lost your leg. I just worry that it pains you still and if so, I might have some salve that would stop the phantom pain that still plagues you. It would be my gift to you for saving my granddaughter."

Knowing it was futile to argue with a woman, he simply smiled just enough that his dimples popped.

"I would be honored to accept some of your salve, Thank You. And no, I have no regrets Moriah. Everything happens for a reason and if I hadn't lost my leg, I'd still be serving and wouldn't have met the love of my life. And wouldn't be here with you at this very moment. So no, no I don't have any regrets."

"Then you are as wise as you are easy on the eye Doctor. Our Nicole is very lucky to have had you enter her life just when she had given up. And I thank you for saving her, in more ways that even you realize. Because of you, our girl is about to come full circle."

Not quite sure of her choice of words, Aedan took in what she said but didn't respond.

"What could this woman know of Nicole as she had met her just briefly," he wondered. Before he could ask, Nicole appeared in the doorway.

"Is that coffee I smell? Oh my God, I don't like coffee but definitely need some caffeine," she said, reaching for his outstretched arm.

"Your tea has been steeping Nicole, and should be ready for you."

Surprised, Nicole looked up. "You made me tea? How did you know I love tea?"

"Danielle mentioned it a time or two. I'll be right back with it."

As Moriah disappeared into her kitchen, Nicole stretched and smiled at the man who'd slowly ingrained his way into her heart and had become her best friend. "Good morning."

"Good morning gorgeous," he responded back, smiling just enough to allow his dimples to come out.

As Moriah handed her a steaming mug of Earl Grey tea, Nicole graciously accepted it and asked about how their patient had done during the night, although she somehow already knew the answer.

"She slept well and the fever is much lower, thanks to your medicine. We owe you her life and we are forever indebted to you. Your actions will not be forgotten and when the time comes, know that we will be here for you as well. You both are welcome in our homes and in our community anytime, and your sister as well Aedan."

Nicole and Aedan exchanged glances and Aedan couldn't help to wonder what the elder's somewhat cryptic messages were all about but Nicole just accepted her gratitude as just that, gratitude and her unusual choice of words didn't faze her at all. Her heart warmed in hearing the good news about her little friend as she sipped on her tea.

"Well then, let's get on over to check our girl out. I think she's going to be up and moving a lot better by day's end."

The walk over to Star's home took less than a minute and as soon as they entered, Nicole could feel that the energy had changed in the tiny home. Making her way into the child's bedroom, she found Star still sitting at the head of her daughter's bed, brushing her long black hair. She looked exhausted but kept stroking the child's head over and over, as if trying to raise her from her sleep. Star's husband stood ever silent observing the invasion of people into his home, knowing that even though he did not want them there, it was futile to argue with an estrogen filled room of women. He did not like the other man in the room. He had no reason to dislike him, but he did not trust nor want this man in his house or near his women. But again, he knew enough to keep his thoughts and opinions to himself.

Nicole quickly hung the third dose of antibiotics into the slowly dripping IV, noting that the site was still patent, and Rainie's vital signs were much improved from the day before. Her heart was no longer racing and now within a normal range for a preteen, and her breathing was much less labored. Feeling her forehead, she still had a slight temperature, but was no longer burning up like she had been when they'd arrive yesterday afternoon. She continued to talk to Rainie as if the child was awake and taking part in the conversation. As she started talking about her beloved dogs, she felt a slight tug on her pant leg and nearly jumped when she realized that it was Rainie pulling on her clothing. The movement was noted by everyone in the room, with everyone quickly gathering around the child. Nicole leaned in closer to the child's face.

"Well Miss Rainie, do you have something you'd like to say about my pups as well? I love my boys very much and would love to know what you think of them," she said, encouraging the girl to finally break out of her state.

As if summoning all her strength, she never opened her eyes, but whispered softly "Neiko is beautiful. But I love Sinjin and want a dog like him someday, but daddy says no."

Keeping her composure, even though she was bursting with tears, Nicole calmly responded to the semiconscious girl.

"Tell you what Rainie, how about you let your grandmother's and my medicine work, and once you're feeling better, you and your family can all come over and visit with Sinjin okay? But you need to rest now and let your body get stronger okay? I've got to clean the wound on your leg now, and I know that it's not going to feel very good and it might hurt you a lot Rainie. But I need for you to be brave. Be brave like my Sinjin is okay?"

"I'll be brave," and with that, the child was back asleep again.

Nicole cleansed the raw areas of the wound as gently as she could, with Aedan noting the improvement already. It appeared that their antibiotics were working. Once the medication had infused and Nicole had finished redressing the wound, they stopped the intravenous fluids, leaving the heplock in her hand to be used later in the afternoon. Nicole informed both Rainie's parents and also her grandmother that she would be back in the afternoon after she finished up at the clinic and hopefully after another days' worth of IV antibiotics, they might be able to switch her over to oral antibiotics if she kept improving. Nicole promised to return with more dressing supplies and return as soon as she could break away from the clinic.

Star's husband, who had remained somewhat aloof to the unwanted visitors, offered to show them back to the river with Aedan politely declining. Nicole couldn't help but notice the tension escalate when the two men conversed. She didn't want to read anything into it, other than the fact that they were two strong willed men seeing who had the most testosterone. Once ready to leave, they exited the tiny home to find their horses saddled up and waiting for them. The teenager holding the reins could have passed for Bruce's double but was obviously years younger than Danielle's fiancée. Nicole looked into the piercing black eyes of the child trying so hard to be a man and smiled.

"Thank You very much young man. I'm Nicole and I don't believe we've met."

"Um, I'm Caleb. Your horses are ready and have been fed and watered.

"Thank You very much Caleb. We, and I'm sure, the horses, appreciate you taking such good care of them. Do you like horses?" she asked innocently, continuing the conversation as Aedan grew impatient.

"Um, yes. Actually I do. I love to ride when there's time. And Danielle's horses are pretty astounding, especially the stallion."

Interrupting, Aedan who was already abreast the stallion being discussed, coughed gently to get their attention.

"Nicole, we really need to get moving if we're going to get home, shower and be at the clinic within the hour."

Realizing that he was right, she smiled at her new young friend and promised they'd continue their conversation sometime in the near future. She mounted the mare waiting patiently for her and nodded to Aedan that she was ready for the quick ride back to the river and to their cabin.

Chapter 26

Aedan had no trouble following the well-worn trail leading to the water and before they knew it, they were at the river's edge. Being so early in the morning, the fall air remained crisp and unforgiving as they slowly navigated their reluctant horses into the nearly waist deep current. They didn't wat the horses exposed to the cold water any longer than necessary, so Nicole encouraged her ride to move faster and within a minute, they were exiting the water and heading up the last remaining slope to the warmth of Danielle's barn. As if clairvoyant, Danielle pushed open the doors allowing them entry inside. Immediately upon dismounting the horses, both she and Bruce removed the saddles and proceeded to wipe down the horses, who didn't seem to even notice the frigid air temperature. Dying for a shower and another cup of tea, Nicole excused herself once her horse was attended to, and practically ran across the yard to her truck, leaving Aedan to fend for himself. Danielle promised to run him back once they finished up with the horses, and he updated her on Rainie's condition. The last thing she heard before she left was him yelling something about not using up all of the hot water.

She had barely opened the front door before she was stampeded by two very happy dogs. She crouched down to accept all of their licks, paw shakes, and doggie kisses. After giving them each their entire quota of biscuits for the day, Nicole made her way into the shower to wash away the aches and pains brought on by sleeping on such a hard surface the night before. And determined to not be shown up by her roommate, she was washed, dried and dressed for the workday by the time Aedan entered their cabin. She smiled to herself upon seeing his expression when he realized that she was nearly ready for the clinic. She'd done some kind of weird twist with her auburn hair, leaving a few strands falling gently against her naked neck.

"God she is beautiful and doesn't even know it," he thought to himself as he dropped the backpack on the chair and told her he'd be in and out of the shower in three minutes, ready to go in 5. And he was.

Feeling guilty for leaving the dogs alone all evening and night, Nicole insisted on bringing them into the clinic for the day. Neiko was his typical well-mannered self. Sinjin, on the other hand, quickly realized that he enjoyed being the center of attention as he darted in and out of the waiting room, with the staff chasing after him. The patients in attendance chuckled watching the fiasco unfolding in front of them. Nicole didn't seem fazed at all but Miranda was not interested in having a "wild mutt" disrupting their day. Feeling that the two opinionated women's exchange might escalate, Aedan quickly offered to take the pup off both of their hands by calling his sister to the rescue. Danielle and Bruce entered the crowded waiting room and were greeted warmly by everyone in attendance. One thing about small communities, whether appreciated or not, everyone knows everyone. And it didn't take long for the whispering to start upon seeing Bruce. Many of the old timers in attendance remembered him as the scrawny, half-starved teenager when he'd first appeared in their town, searching for a life different than the one he'd left behind at the tender age of sixteen. He'd crossed the river originally in search of his aunt whom he thought lived in their town, and had stayed because he had nowhere else to go. He lived on the streets for a few cold nights, eventually being taken in by the post master's widow. She'd immediately felt a warm spot for him. She gave him a roof above his head, and three square meals a day, but also made him earn his keep. In the two years that he lived with her, he earned her trust, admiration and love. She insisted that he finish his education, and having never attended a public school before, he was at first terrified but quickly came to love school in a way he never thought possible. His mind was like a sponge, absorbing everything presented to him.

Bruce never forgot the woman who became a second mother to him, and even after he'd moved out to be on his own upon graduating from technical school, he called her daily and visited her at least once a week, always remembering to bring her a bouquet of flowers. Now, years later, he still dropped by weekly to bring her flowers or simply to chat with the woman who'd taught him how to be a man. Danielle accompanied him often to her final resting spot, where Bruce's surrogate mother was interned next to her husband of forty years. Wishing that she'd had a chance to meet the woman who'd taught her man how to love unselfishly and how to treat a woman with respect and dignity, Danielle always silently whispered "Thank You" before departing the cemetery.

Chapter 27

"Hey Danny. Hi Bruce," Nicole said, over the noise in the waiting room.

"You here to rescue my dogs from these mean patients?" she said as she winked at the three children crouched together on the floor playing with the two bundles of fur who were presently upside down enjoying their belly rubs.

"Yeah, I figured Miranda has had just about enough of your boys for one morning," Bruce said, smiling at his longtime friend who currently was beyond pissed off.

"Oh no Bruce, please leave them. I've so enjoyed having those adorable four legged angels keep me company all morning long, especially when the smaller one felt the need to join me in the john this morning. Took his little nose and pushed the door right open, when I was in all my glory sitting on the pot."

"Her," Bruce responded, still smiling and trying very hard to contain his laughter.

"What?" Miranda asked, now thoroughly exasperated.

"Her. Sinjin didn't use his nose. She used "her" nose. Sinjin's a girl."

"I don't give a #$%@ what he or she is! Just get those damn dogs out of here Bruce!"

"Relax my friend; Nic didn't mean any harm. She just felt guilty for being away from them so long when she was across the river helping Star's daughter."

"How's she doing Bruce?" she asked sympathetically, suddenly forgetting about the ciaos the dogs had been creating. Danielle stood by silently watching the body language between the two longtime friends.

"How were you received when you showed up? It must have been hard on you going back. Was it your first time back since you left?" she asked gently.

"Yeah, but it was okay. No one really had a problem with me being there. Rainie's health was their main focus. Most didn't really say anything. Sort of like I was a ghost and not really there ya know."

Danielle's heart broke listening to the inflection in his voice, and only now fully realizing what her lover had given up when he made the decision to abandon his roots all those years ago.

"I know," Miranda said, her voice emitting empathy, but never sympathy for the man standing in front of her. Knowing his pride would never allow sympathy, she just looked the man that had once meant more to her than her own family, and smiled.

Finally breaking the silence, Danielle spoke up.

"Okay guys, it's time to say good bye to the nice people of the clinic and get you two home where you belong."

Nicole said her good byes to her pups as she called the next patient, a very spry 99 year old woman named Mabel Hodges, into the exam room. Mabel, it seemed, appeared to suffer from gout whether it was 80 or 18 out; and visited the clinic monthly like clockwork. Nicole smiled as she waited for the slightly hunched over woman to get out of her chair and join her, but not before taking the time to tap each dog on the head and sneak them each a treat. Once Nicole and Mrs. Hodges disappeared out of sight, Bruce and Danielle quickly made their escape with the wayward dogs. Once in the truck, Danielle turned toward Bruce and simply said, "I'm sorry Bruce. I'm sorry for all the pain you must have went through as a child and I'm sorry for you having to relive it all over again. I'm sorry for the stupid rules, laws or whatever the hell your former community called them, and I'm sorry that you drove over there and had to feel that pain all over again. If I had known, I would never have allowed you or agreed to you driving over there Bruce. I didn't know."

"She's my niece Danny, and you couldn't have stopped me. They don't acknowledge me as family anymore; but Rainie is, and will always be my niece, and nothing could have stopped me from getting to her if she needed me. We share the same blood and whether they give a rat's ass about me or not, I'm still her uncle. Don't be hard on Star and Moriah when you see them again. They still live in the community and therefore they must follow the sanctions that they've grown up with. Whether you or I agree with their rules doesn't matter. It's their belief and customs and therefore, a code that they must follow because all societies must have some form or structure; otherwise it wouldn't survive. Anyways, enough on them. I'm just so glad to hear that Rainie's starting to come around."

"Her father seems like a piece of work," Danielle added. "Do you think he'll ever let her cross the river to come help us in the greenhouse again after this?"

"He was never one of my favorite people. I nearly killed him before I left for good," Bruce said matter of factly, but in an almost whisper. "Therefore I am not one of his favorite people. Saw him take his hand to my sister, and I nearly broke his neck. If Star hadn't pleaded for his life, he'd have been dead years ago. No, I'm not going to discuss it. All I'll say is that I told him if he ever, and I meant ever, laid a hand on her or what comes from her, I would find out and he would die. Period."

"Oh baby. Again, I'm sorry. But you did the right thing."

"Danny, you're my family now. Always remember that. But, Star and Moriah are still my flesh and blood and I would do anything, risk anything for them. And that includes little Rainie as well."

"My love," Danielle said, rubbing his back as they started down the road and away from the clinic. "You have the temperament of a warrior, but you are one of the kindest men that I've ever known. And," she said, wiping a tear from her eye, "I cannot wait to become your wife someday. I love with every ounce of my heart. And, my love, I will be your family, now and forever okay?"

He reached over, patting her thigh, "Sounds like a plan."

Chapter 28

The rest of the day flew by for everyone at the clinic. Nicole had been under the assumption all day that she was going to return to Star's home independently to give her daughter her next dose of antibiotics, so she was somewhat surprised when Aedan met her in their break room with the supplies they'd need for the child's dressing change and next doses of meds.

"Hey, some of the ladies from the church ran us over some sandwiches," he said, smiling coyly, allowing his dimples to show. "What type of soda would you like me to pack? Or do you just want a water bottle?"

"Water is fine Aedan; but what are you doing? You're needed here and I am perfectly fine riding over to Star's on my own. Or if it makes you happier, I can ask Danny to escort me okay? You are needed here so it only makes sense that I go solo."

"Nope. Miranda's got everything under control here and we're nearly all done seeing patients so I'm coming with you. Like it or not lady, we're a team and we go there as a team. And that's non-negotiable," he added for good measure.

"God you're stubborn," was her only response. But deep down, she breathed a sigh of relief to not have to navigate the river on her own.

"Alright then," he said, surprised that she'd given in so easily.

"I'll be ready when you are and I'll tell Danielle to get the horses saddled up. Or would you prefer that Bruce give us a lift in his truck?"

"No, it's so much faster if we go by horseback so let me change my clothes quickly and I'll be ready."

"Okay, I'll do the same. Oh, and Nicole," he said, still smiling, "I'm so proud to have you as my partner. And I know our little friend will be okay. Hopefully today's doses will be the last IV doses she needs and we can switch her to something oral in the am. I spoke with Danny and Bruce and they'll take care of the dogs again tonight since I doubt I can persuade you to come home after her afternoon dose right?"

"Right. I'm not going anywhere Doc. You're stuck with me," she said, as she left the room to change out of her scrubs and into street clothes.

"And being stuck with you Nicole Rose Brentwood would make me the happiest man alive," he thought as he too stepped away to change.

Chapter 29

The ride across the river seemed shorter this time for them as they now felt more comfortable with crossing the current downstream. Once they'd exited the water, they picked up their pace and headed toward the woods and Moriah's community. Their horses hadn't taken five paces towards the woods before they were met by two men from the community, teenagers really. Having never seen them before, Aedan protectively put his horse between Nicole and the strangers. Sensing his immediate distrust, the older brother spoke up.

"If you're the doctor, I'm Gideon and we were sent to make sure you got here okay."

Still slightly leery, Aedan sized up the two lanky teenagers in front of him. Nicole, on the other hand, greeted them warmly.

"Thank you very much Gideon. I'm Nicole, and we certainly appreciate a little guidance through your woods. The path is well worn but there are many off shoots so I'm glad you're here to help us. How is our little patient doing?"

"I haven't heard mam. My pa just told us to come get you and make sure you made it safely. These woods can be pretty treacherous and people have a tendency to get lost and sometimes disappear in them."

Feeling only slightly unnerved by the teenager's statement, Nicole smiled while Aedan remained silent.

"Alright then, bring us to Rainie. And thank you again for guiding us."

As they made their way into the community, Aedan deduced that they had been expected. Mothers, children, and whatever men who weren't still in the fields or at work; all watched their approach. Always hating to be the center of attention, Nicole quickly dismounted as soon as they were in front of Star's home. She handed the reins to the still silent boy standing beside Gideon and smiled.

"Would you take care of my horse for me?" she asked, revealing a bright smile. Gideon reached over and took the reins before the younger boy could answer.

"He doesn't talk. He's Joshua, my younger brother. Hasn't talked since he was really young," he added.

The boy averted direct eye contact with Nicole and shifted his stance from leg to leg nervously. Nicole crouched down to nearly eye level with the younger boy and again smiled, extending out her hand.

"It's okay if you don't talk Joshua; I usually talk enough for two people. And it's very nice to meet you," she said as she reached her hand into her pocket, pulling out two sugar cubes and passing them to him.

"Do you think you could do me a favor and give these two treats to the horses once they've cooled down? It would really be a great help to me if you'd water them and then give them a little attention."

Knowing that the child might be nonverbal but obviously understood everything that she was saying when he looked her directly in the eyes, smiled slightly while grabbing the sugar cubes out of her hand. Nicole proceeded to talk to the boy as if they were having a two-way conversation as his older brother and Aedan looked on, somewhat impatiently.

"Joshua, the big guy that Aedan, I mean, the Doctor was riding is Zeus. Isn't he beautiful? And this girl," she said, patting the side of her ride, "is Lucretia, Cree for short. She's just as beautiful as the stallion, but can be pretty temperamental and stubborn. You take good care of them for me okay?"

Saying nothing, but revealing a bigger grin, the boy looked her directly in the eyes and nodded as he grabbed the reins from his brother and led the horses away. Before entering Star's home, Nicole thanked Gideon as well, then quickly entered the opened door leading to her patient.

Chapter 30

Aedan and Nicole made their way back to the child's room where they found Moriah still at the Rainie's side. Her father stood off in the shadows while Star spoke.

"She has been awake on and off all day, taking sips of water and juice like you instructed us to do when she was awake. We got a lot in her," she said as she lifted up a well-worn glass showing the size of what the child had consumed.

"But she hasn't eaten anything. She needs to eat something to get better."

Knowing how hard it was for lay people to understand the concept of not eating, Nicole gently reassured her that Rainie wouldn't get dehydrated and malnourished by not eating for a few days and the IV was providing her with essential nutrients until she was strong enough to eat again. Nicole checked her IV site to make sure it wasn't infiltrated prior to hanging the next dose of antibiotic. Aedan checked the child's blood pressure as she slept and carefully pulled up her pajama leg to reveal the dressing on her injured leg. Once the antibiotic was hung and the rest of her vital signs were checked, Nicole started talking to the sleeping child.

"Rainie, oh Miss Rainbow, its Nicole. Doctor Aedan and I are back again to give you that special medicine to make you stronger and better. I need you to wake up for us okay, and tell us how you're feeling. Your fever's almost gone so I know you must be feeling a lot better. Let's wake up so that your momma and daddy can talk to you and see for themselves that you're going to be back to normal real soon, okay sweetie."

Nicole gently shook the child's shoulder to arouse her. "And I'm going to need to change the dressing on my leg soon Rainie so I need you to be a big brave girl okay? Can you do that for me?"

With eyes still partially closed, the child spoke.

"Nicki, did you bring the puppies with you? I want to play with Sinjin," the child said softly, still foggy and half out of it. Nicole felt a lump in the back of her throat as she smiled and replied.

"Ah baby, I came right from the clinic so I couldn't bring the boys, but if it's okay with your parents," she said as she looked at both of Rainie's parents.

"If you wake up and eat something for them tonight, I'll bring Sinjin and Neiko back with me tomorrow when I come by to check on you. Would that be alright with you?"

She looked directly at Rainie's father and stared directly at him, refusing to be intimidated by his glare. He did not answer but realizing she was unwavering, reluctantly nodded yes. Smiling in triumph, Nicole jostled Rainie slightly harder to make her stir. "Rainie honey, your daddy said that Sinjin can come and play with you tomorrow; so I really need you to try and wake up now, and after we do your dressing change, I'll have your momma bring you something warm to sip on and eat okay?"

Hearing her cue, Star rushed off to the kitchen to warm up the lentil soup that she had on the stovetop. As Aedan started gently unwrapping the dressing on the child's leg, he noted her father easing forward. Not sure how he'd respond, if at all, he looked up and requested more than asked.

"I really could us help holding your daughter's leg while Nicole irrigates the wound." Not really giving the man an option, Rainie's father reluctantly stepped forward and knelt at his daughter's side. Nicole seized the moment and without making eye contact with the man, pretended she was still fussing with the intravenous, said nonchalantly, "I don't think I remember your name sir; what did you sit was?"

Cornered, he paused a few moments, and then responded. "You can't recall because my name was never offered to you. My name is Ellis."

Smiling, Nicole continued fidgeting with the tubing in her hands.

"Well Ellis, it's very nice meeting you and you have a beautiful daughter here who'll be up and good as new before you know it."

"You are not welcome here. You are not like us."

Hearing the words, Moriah spoke for the first time since their arrival.

"Hush! These people might not be part of our community the way that you and I are, but they are welcome here anytime and whether you admit it or not, we both know that Nicole is more like us than she is not. Please disregard what my stubborn son-in-law has said. You and what will come from you, or any of the family that helped raise you are welcome here and are to join our community when the time comes."

Having absolutely no clue what the elderly woman was talking about, Nicole just mouthed "Thank You," and proceeded to gently remove the dressing on Rainie's leg. After unwrapping the first few layers of kerlix gauze, Nicole had to start irrigating the dressing with saline to loosen up the areas adhering to the wound. Rainie squirmed from the pain but remained as still and cooperative as possible. Seeing that his daughter was in pain, Ellis, for the first time that Nicole had witnessed, spoke soothingly and tenderly in a tongue foreign to both she and Aedan. The child nodded and slowly opened her eyes and looked directly into Nicole's green eyes and penetrated her soul.

"Promise me you'll bring Sinjin tomorrow Miss Nicole," she half asked, half said.

"I promise Miss Rainbow Elizabeth."

"I'm hungry I think. Daddy said I have to get well soon so I can play with your mutt. I told him Sinjin is not a mutt, but a brave girl like me!"

Feeling the tears in her eyes, Nicole simply smiled. "Yes she is Rainie. She's brave like you. You and my Sinjin are both brave fighters."

And with that, the child didn't move as her dressing was changed and redressed. The wound already looked less inflamed and even her father commented on how much better it was looking, thanks in part to their medicine. Aedan reassured him that it truly had been a combination of old world, and modern medicine that had saved his daughter's life and together, they had made a difference and sometimes working together was the only way to achieve a goal. Rainie's father pondered on the statement and surprising even himself, he stared back at the former soldier now standing shoulder to shoulder with him, and extended out his hand.

"Thank you for saving my daughter's life. You and your woman's actions will never be forgotten."

Aedan looked over at Nicole and smiled, hearing her referred to as "his woman." "You're welcome Ellis."

Nicole no sooner had the dressing replaced on Rainie's leg, when the child slowly started pushing herself up into a sitting position. Star gasped as she saw the first independent movement of her daughter in days. As she nearly dropped the bowl of soup that she was carrying, she couldn't help but start to cry as her only child looked up at her and smiled.

"I need to get better soon momma because Nicole is going to bring Sinjin over to play with me tomorrow, right Nicole?" she asked, through a big grin.

"And I'm really hungry now momma," she added as an afterthought.

Everyone sat at Rainie's bedside as she ate with Nicole frequently reminding her to take small sips of the soup to avoid getting a stomach ache. The conversation was light and on various topics from gardening, Danielle's horses, where Nicole and Aedan had grown up and how they had met. Everything laughed as Aedan joked about Nicole blowing him off on top of a mountain in the Adirondacks when they originally met, and thinking that Danielle, his twin, was his girlfriend. Even Ellis burst out in full blown laughter as Aedan told the story of their reunion and Nicole nearly running him over with her truck and camping trailer. When the conversation waned, Nicole casually asked who had sent Gideon and Joshua to them to help them make it to the village, to which Star answered.

"Ellis asked his nephews to meet you at the river."

Surprised, Nicole continued the conversation. "Thank you. They both seem like very nice young men, and were very gracious in taking our horses and caring for them once we got here. They are your nephews Ellis? Do you have a big family?" she asked innocently.

"Yes they are my nephews," was all he offered, avoiding any questions about his family. The nurse in Nicole couldn't let the subject drop.

"Gideon said that Joshua used to talk as a toddler but no longer speaks?" When Ellis didn't answer, it was Moriah who spoke up.

"Yes, our little Joshua used to talk nonstop when he was about three or four. But then the accident happened to his parents, and he hasn't spoken a word since."

Knowing she was a guest in their home, and shouldn't push the issue, she asked anyways. "Accident?"

Moriah looked over at her son-in-law, who appeared to be lost in his own thoughts, and responded.

"Yes, Ellis's sister was crossing the river on horseback, heading into your town. Even though her husband had discouraged her from going, she insisted that your store had what she needed. She had Joshua with her. Her husband and older son Gideon were working along the riverbank checking their traps when they heard the scream." Seeing Ellis' posture change, Moriah continued on.

"Ana's horse had lost its footing and stumbled in the strong current, throwing both she and Joshua into the churning water. Abe commanded Gideon to summon help as he rushed into the frigid water to rescue his family. No one really knows what happened after that. Moments later, when Gideon returned with several men to assist in the rescue, they found Joshua on the shore crying and both Ana and Abraham face down in the water. Speculation has it that Abe got his son to safety but died trying to rescue his beloved Ana, and Joshua witnessed the whole thing. And he hasn't spoken a word since."

"That poor baby," Nicole said, feeling the child's anguish. "It's no wonder the child doesn't speak. Witnessing something that horrific would traumatize anyone. He lost two of the most important people in his life and he saw it happen in front of him. That is awful."

"Actually," Moriah responded, "He lost three; for Ana was pregnant at the time of her death and Joshua had been so excited about the prospect of a new sister or brother. Gideon doesn't talk about it much, and everyone treats Joshua as if he still talked. It's been years now, so for the most part, it's just accepted."

"If they lost both parents," Nicole asked, "Who is raising them?"

"They live with Ellis's other sister, but unlike other communities, everyone in our village looks out for all of the children and takes care of them regardless who they belong too. Our entire village help raise the generations that will carry on our ways after we're gone."

Aedan and Nicole absorbed information that had been divulged to them. Both being orphans to a degree, Nicole at birth, and Aedan as a teenager, they both understood, to a degree, what the poor child must have endured at such a young age. Once Rainie was finished with her soup, Aedan asked Nicole to join him outside so that he could discuss something with her. She quickly obliged and once outside, once alone, he kissed her. She said nothing about them being in public, and melted into his kiss which lasted just long enough to enjoy. When she pulled away, she asked if that was his reason for them excusing themselves to which he laughed.

"No, actually I wanted your opinion. I was thinking since Rainie is responding so well to the IV antibiotic, and her leg is already looking significantly less inflamed, that maybe after tomorrow's dose in the morning, we can switch her to an oral version. What do you think? It certainly would be a lot easier on everyone if she was taking pills."

She thought about her response for a moment or two.

"I think that you are probably right, but let's plan on waiting and seeing what tomorrow brings before we say anything to Rainie or her parents. I would hate to get their hopes up, only to disappoint them. Besides, I have to bring the pups over tomorrow afternoon after work anyways. I promised remember?"

"Yeah I remember. I'll arrange for Bruce to bring us back here in his truck tomorrow because we sure as hell aren't bringing the dogs on horseback."

Knowing he was right, she agreed without argument.

Once the antibiotic as completed, Nicole flushed the IV line and heparinized it so it'd be patent for the next dose due at midnight. As they'd done the previous night, they headed over to Moriah's home to spend the evening and catch some sleep before the next administration. They made small talk, but like the night before, fatigue set in quickly and they retired for a few hours' sleep. They repeated the routine again at midnight and at 7am before heading across the river and back to their cabin for a quick shower and another day at the clinic.

Miranda, though not a warm and fuzzy kind of girl, nor a good cook by any stretch of the imagination, had a full spread waiting for them when they arrived at the clinic with only minutes to spare before the first patient was scheduled to be seen. When they attempted to thank her for the amazing meal, she quickly fluffed it off, stating that she'd had a lot of help and that much of it had been donated by other women. Aedan saw right through her tough exterior and pulled her into a bear hug and gave her one of his killer dimpled grins. Shooing him away, she feigned exasperation, but both Nicole and Aedan knew that it was all for show for the other staff members in attendance. They dove in and inhaled as much as they could before they started another full day at the clinic. The day flew by much like the previous ones but nearly every patient who came today asked them, complimented them or thanked them for what they'd done for Rainie. Surprised that word had spread from one side of the river to the other, Nicole quickly

realized that though their cultures, customs and way of life might be vastly different from one another; they were in fact, still neighboring communities and in such, probably were more similar than they realized. Moriah herself had said that they came sometimes came across the river to frequent Mystique's stores, and several of the women came faithfully every Saturday to work in the greenhouses.

"They need a bridge."

Realizing that she wasn't talking to herself, and in fact was speaking to him, Aedan looked up at Nicole as they closed up at the end of the day. "What?"

"I said, they need a bridge over the river. They need a safer, easier way to connect the two communities."

"Do not go there Nicole. There is a reason that it's so challenging getting over to Moriah's village. They want it that way, and it's not our place to start telling them that they need this or they need that. They barely trust us as it is and tolerate us only because we're providing a service that they couldn't accomplish themselves. Please don't open up a can of worms or offend those people by telling them what they may or may not need. I know," he said, pulling her into his arms and kissing her gently on the forehead, "that you have nothing but the best of intentions, but please don't ruffle any feathers, okay?"

"I won't honey," she responded as he held her tightly. What he didn't see were the crossed fingers behind her back as she said it.

Bruce pulled into the drive at exactly 3:30pm to find both Aedan and Nicole changed and waiting for him. They said their goodbyes to their staff and jumped into the cab of his truck, only to be greeted by two wound up dogs that were extremely happy to see them. After giving them both attention, kisses and pats on the head, Nicole settled in for the bumpy arduous drive down the unmarked dirt roads into Moriah's village.

"What is the name of their community Bruce? It just dawned on me that we don't even know the name of their town. Shit, how do they even get mail I wonder?" she continued once they were underway. "It's not like they get mail daily out there in the middle of nowhere. I sincerely doubt that the mailman makes that trip daily or crosses the river to bring them their cable or utility bills right? God, I had never thought of that before, how exactly do they function like other normal towns when they live in such a desolate, isolated area?"

Laughing, he simply shook his head and mouthed to Bruce, "There she goes again."

"Screw you both," she said, half in jest as they both burst out laughing at her expense.

Aedan conversed with both Nicole and Bruce during the ride back into Bruce's home town, all the while remaining cognizant of the turns that Bruce was making along the way. None of the roads were marked, yet Aedan memorized every turn to memory. What he didn't realize was that Nicole was doing the same thing, even though she simply appeared to be playing with her four legged friends during the ride.

Turning onto the last remaining road before reaching their village, Bruce finally spoke. "Destiny; the town is called Destiny. I have no idea how, why or when it was named that, but even though there is no office post office in town, those that live there still are legally recognized as being residents of Destiny, New Hampshire. And here we are entering the big metropolis of Destiny now."

Nicole smiled as she saw the town coming into view, even though it was a part of town that neither she nor Aedan had ever seen before. Bruce navigated the roads as if he drove them daily and before they realized it, he was putting the truck into park in front of his sister's home. Star met them at the door with a bright smile, and quickly hugged her only brother.

"Come in my friends, I think you'll be very surprised at what you find," she said in a voice radiating hope.

The three of them hurried in, but followed Star not to Rainie's, but to a small but immaculate sunroom in the back of the home overlooking their massive garden. They found Rainie and her grandmother on a loveseat together reading a book and chuckling over a secret only known to them. When Rainie looked up and realized that she had company, she beamed with initial excitement but her radiant smile very quickly turned to a frown.

"I thought that you were bringing the puppies with you" she asked, trying to conceal her disappointment but failing miserably.

Wanting to tease her just a little, Aedan nonchalantly responded back to their young patient, as he winked at Moriah who could tell by his response that he was just kidding.

"The pups. Oh shoot, I knew there was something we forgot to bring with us Nicole. Oh sorry kid, we didn't think you'd be awake and up to playing with them so we left them at home; sorry about that."

Trying very hard to conceal her disappointment, Rainie squared her shoulders. "That's okay. Maybe you can bring them next time you come visit us."

Seeing her lip quivering, Bruce quickly excused himself and returned less than a minute later. Not wanting his poor niece to suffer any longer, he slowly opened the door to the sunroom and softly called her name. Once he had her attention, he opened the door wide open and in bounded eight furry legs carrying two very happy and excited dogs. They raced into the sunroom, with Neiko immediately going to Nicole's side and the pup running between everyone present but once she saw Rainie, she went right to her side, practically climbing up onto her lap. Even Ellis and Star couldn't deny how incredibly happy their only child looked nuzzled up with the small dog. Star, who had never had a dog of her own either, made her way to her daughter's side, holding out her hand for the slightly hyper dog to sniff. Impressed on how well behaved the lanky looking pup was, she asked how long Nicole had had her. Nicole proceeded to tell Sinjin's story and how she acquired her. Rainie and Sinjin sat side by side as Nicole told her tale and Aedan gently unwrapped the dressing on her leg. Pleased with how the wound was healing, he knew that her mother or grandmother could continue with the daily dressing changes until her wound was healed. Star and Moriah both quickly agreed that they could perform the daily dressing change and once it was redressed, Rainie quickly got up and asked if she could bring the puppy outside. Confident that neither dog would wander too far from the home, Nicole quickly agreed but spoke to her beloved Shepherd first. "Essere un bravo ragazzo e non lo vagare troppo lontano. E mantenere la nostra ragazza al sicuro."

Moriah, Star, and Ellis all appeared confused by Nicole's command in an unknown language. Not sure what to make of it, Moriah looked to her son for answers. "What language does our guest speak? It was not German though her dog is."

Bruce chuckled. "No Moriah, that would only make sense, wouldn't it? Our Nicole taught her German dog to speak Italian, isn't that crazy?" he said, with a smile. "Darn dog acts like he understands every blessed word she says too; that's the kicker."

"I think our Nicole is wise beyond her years and full of all sorts of surprises. I just hope she's ready for all the surprises that will enter her life in the near future."

"Momma, what do you know that you're not telling us? Nicole and Aedan are some of my closest friends. So please, if you know something that could hurt them or alter their lives, please tell me or them, so we can stop it or fix it."

"Mein Sohn, wissen Sie, wir das Schicksal nicht andern. Our destiny has already been predetermined and there is nothing that any of us can do to change it. That my son is why it's called fate. And we must accept what is and what's meant to be."

"Like you just accepted it when I left momma? Yes, I left willingly, but momma," Bruce said, almost in a near whisper, "I thought after a few days that maybe you'd come for me. I was alone, in a world not my own, with no money, nowhere to sleep and nothing to eat and I was scared. And I missed you and dad and Star almost as soon as I left. Why didn't you come for me?" he asked, almost pleading.

"My heart broke when I learned that you'd left. The light in my eyes and in my soul has never been the same since that day seventeen years ago. But you chose your destiny and it was not for me to alter your path, just as it wasn't for me to alter Arla's when she left either. She was my sister, my best friend and confident and part of me died when she left all those years before you; but her wild spirit could never be tamed, much as yours could never either. I had the honor of raising you for your first sixteen years and I have silently thanked the woman who became for second mother every day since she took you in. I owe that woman more than I could ever tell her, and you are the man that you've become because of her and the life that she gave you. I have never told you this before my son; but I am very proud of you and if your father were still alive, he'd tell you the same thing.

Suddenly realizing something that had plagued him for years; he looked into the eyes of his birth mother. "You're the one aren't you? You're the one who's planted the fresh flowers on her grave every spring, the blue bonnets and the Shasta daisies? It was you wasn't it momma?"

Blushing only slightly, and wishing she could deny it but refusing to lie to her only son, Moriah looked up.

"I had to thank her somehow and didn't know any other way. I went to visit her once before she passed you know," she said softly, catching the attention of her daughter and son-in-law. "You were at school at the time. She said that you were about to graduate from school and had been accepted into technical school. She beamed as she spoke your name, and it was evident that she loved you very much. We ate lunch at the very table where you shared dinner with her every night and I could feel your presence even if you weren't there. Yes, it was destiny that you left me but fate that you found her, and I will always be indebted to her," she said, silently wiping a lone tear from her face. Looking over at Nicole and Aedan, she added one last comment, aimed directly at Nicole.

"Just because one mother lets a child go doesn't mean that part of her heart doesn't go with them or that she didn't love that child. It simply means that she's hoping that whatever fate has in store for her child is grander, bigger and more spectacular than anything that she could have offered the child. Sometimes we just have to be patient to understand why things happen. Everything in nature happens for a reason and in the end, everything comes full circle; we just have to be patient. If I didn't believe that, then I would not have the honor of my only son being here with us now," she finished, opening her arms to embrace her long lost son.

"It took almost losing my granddaughter to gain a son."

"Oh momma, I have missed you so."

Bruce's massive frame enveloped Moriah's petite weathered body as he hugged her lovingly.

"And I know I'm not part of the community anymore and not welcome here anymore but please, please remember that you are welcome to come visit Danielle and I anytime you want, for as long as you want. Now that she knows we're family, she'll be hounding you at every opportunity, so that she can get to know you better. You might as well get together with her soon and chat because I tell you; she's relentless when she latches onto something."

Aedan laughed listening to Bruce's very accurate description of his twin, knowing that he'd described her exactly how she was.

"Whether you are still part of this community or not Bruce," Aedan spoke up, I know my sister and she will definitely want to get to know her future mother-in-law a lot better now that she knows your real identity," he said with a smile. "She might be my twin, but she is definitely more stubborn and persuasive than me, and she will want to get to know you as soon as possible, both you and Star," he added, looking over at Bruce's sister.

"Moriah," Bruce added, choosing his words carefully, Danny and I haven't set an exact wedding date yet, but do you think it's possible that you, Star, Ellis, and of course Rainie, would be able to attend? It would be an honor to have my family present."

"No. They are not your family anymore," Ellis quickly interjected before either Star or Moriah could answer. Immediately feeling the urge to knee the obnoxious man in the balls, Nicole kept her physical reaction to herself but could not hold her tongue any longer.

"Excuse me, but you are a hypocrite! And an idiot and quite frankly, a jackass if I say so myself." Star gasped but Nicole continued on. "Bruce, your brother-in-law whether you chose to admit it or not, made a juvenile if not childish decision at the tender age of 16 to see what life outside of your commune was all about. Moriah is right, our destiny has been predetermined and his was to leave your world to see what the rest of the world had to offer. I cannot speak for him, and have only known him for a brief period of time, but there is one thing that I know for certain, his number one priority has always been taking care of what's his and the ones that he loves. I bet there hasn't been a day that's gone by in the last 17 years that he hasn't had regrets about leaving his parents and his sister and if given the opportunity, he might very well go back in time and never leave on that day so many years ago. But, just because he left, does not mean that his family here, in this town doesn't mean the world to him. And pardon me for saying so, but you are so set on alienating and dismissing anything or anyone from outside your little microcosm of a community but you welcomed us, even though it was reluctantly, when it benefited you didn't you? Granted, it wasn't you who sought us out when your daughter needed more help than you could provide her; but it was you who allowed us to work with you to achieve the same goal. We, Bruce, and the people of Mystique River aren't the enemy you know. You have your rules, lifestyle and customs on this side of the river, and they have theirs. Both communities have little quirks that might seem strange to others, but they are no different than you and your community. Everyone is just trying to survive and live in harmony, and if you don't embrace what Bruce is offering you, then you are a fool! Not everyone gets a second chance, and here and now, your family is getting one. Seize it, embrace it and cherish it. Allow your wife to reconnect with her brother, allow your daughter to get to know her only uncle better, and allow your brother-in-law to learn your customs through you and your people. Everyone will win if you open your minds and open your hearts."

Feeling the tension in the room, Aedan spoke up, trying to relax a stressed atmosphere.

"See, told you she could talk for more than a minute straight, using only one breathe of air. I have absolutely no idea how she does it." And with that, the room burst into laughter, just as Rainie reentered the sunroom with dogs at her feet.

"Oh Daddy, please let me get a puppy someday. Oh please, oh please! I'll take care of him and water and feed him, and take him for walks. I'll brush him and make sure he's quiet at night time; oh please daddy." Seeing his little girl almost back to her old spunky self, the stoic man almost broke down. He crouched down to greet his daughter as she threw herself into his arms.

"Maybe someday we'll get a puppy and give it a trial run. We'll see. It's fall now and no one is having puppies this time of year my precious. We'll probably have to wait until spring to find you a puppy."

Seizing the moment, Nicole coughed gently to gain everyone attention so that she would hopefully have alliances.

"You can borrow my Sinjin. It looks like she already loves your daughter and she is housebroken so she would be a great fit for a trial run."

Knowing that she'd backed him into a corner, Star spoke up before Rainie's squeal of delight got too high. "We can't take your dog Nicole, that wouldn't be right."

"She was never mine Star. Just like your brother Star, it was fate that I found her, but destiny that brought her to Mystique River and to your daughter. I believe that she was given a second chance so that she could enter your daughter's life. Take her, and see how she works out and if it's meant to be, then she is yours..."

Hearing her words, Rainie ran to her father whom she knew would be the harder sell.

"Oh please daddy, can't we at least borrow her from Nicole just for a little bit. I promise, I will do everything for her, take care of her, and she can sleep with me and you'll never even know that she is here. Oh please papa?"

Knowing that all eyes were on him, and waiting for his response, and knowing he'd be judged by his response, he shrugged in defeat.

"I guess it would be okay to keep her for a day or two until you're feeling better." Before he could add any contingencies to his reluctant approval, both Star and Rainie dove into his arms thanking him. As if she understood what was going on, Sinjin ran to Nicole, giving her kisses as if to say good-bye, and just as quickly, ran back to Rainie's side and surprising everyone, went to

Ellis' side and barked to get his attention. When Ellis bent down to the pup's level, the young dog sat and put his paw up as if to say "Hello, and thank you."

Nicole and Aedan both agreed that since Rainie no longer was febrile, and her wound looked significantly better and less inflamed, she would be able to switch from intravenous to oral antibiotics. Nicole gently removed the IV catheter, replacing it with a tiny dressing. He then instructed Star to administer the oral antibiotics every eight hours, making sure she never missed a dose and to take the meds until gone. Moriah and Star promised to monitor the child's temperature daily and to do her dressing changes to her leg as instructed. Rainie was excited about no more needles and the aspect of having her very own dog so she proceeded to agree to whatever Aedan and her parents told her.

Once Nicole made sure that both Sinjin and Rainie were all set, she packed up her supplies and signaled to Bruce that they were ready to get back home. After they said their good byes and both Nicole and Aedan felt confident that Rainie was in good hands with her mother and grandmother, they headed toward the truck with Neiko at their side. Ellis followed them out to Bruce's truck and as they were loading up, he finally spoke what was on his mind.

"You knew the consequences when you made the decision to leave years ago Bruce. Those rules are still in place and still are enforced. But," he said hesitantly, "Maybe there are mitigating circumstances and maybe we should rethink some of our ways. What I'm trying to say," he stammered, "Is that you didn't need to come back here to help us, yet you did. And if it weren't for you, your woman and their," he said, looking directly at Nicole and Aedan, "help; my daughter might not be with us right now. And for that I will be forever in your debt. In all of your debts. And you my brother," he said as he extended his hand, "are welcome in my home and in our community anytime." Taking his hand in his, Bruce shook his brother-in-laws hand and smiled. "Thank you." And with that, they headed back toward Mystique and his waiting woman.

Chapter 31

They rode in silence, all lost in their own thoughts. Once Nicole, Neiko and Aedan were back inside the confines of their own cabin, Aedan pulled her into his arms and told her just one simple statement.

"You did a wonderful thing tonight Nicole and you gave that little girl the most precious gift she could ever receive and I am so proud of you especially knowing how hard that must have been for you. I love you Nicole Brentwood and you never cease to amaze me."

"Her father will let her keep her won't he? Oh God Aedan, what if she falls in love with Sinjin, and her father won't let her keep her? I hadn't thought of that when I offered her the pup. He wouldn't be that cruel would he?"

"Nope, I honestly think that he has a soft spot and that his daughter is his Achilles' heel so to speak. So I don't think he'll make her give the pup away. Are you going to be okay if Sinjin never comes back home?" he asked gingerly.

"Yes. I have definitely come to love that little girl but I'm okay letting her go if she can bring Rainie the kind of joy that my Neiko has brought me. So yes, I can let her go as long as I know she's going to a good home and will be somewhere where she is taken care of and loved and never neglected."

"As I said Ms. Brentwood, you are an amazing woman and I am so proud of you. And I'd love to take you to bed right now if you're remotely interested."

"I believe I'm remotely interested," she said as she smiled and locked the front door and dimmed the lights.

Chapter 32

The remainder of the week went quickly for everyone at the clinic. Word spread quickly about what Aedan and Nicole had done for the people across the river. Several townsfolk offered comments and compliments, opinions and analogies as to why they were allowed passage and acceptance to a degree; none of which Aedan paid much attention to. He and Nicole knew that they were allowed into Moriah's isolated community because they were desperate, and in desperate times, people resort to desperate measures. If allowing strangers into their village was what they had to do to save one of their own, so be it. Nicole missed her pup but knew that she'd done the right thing and in knowing that, the pain was lessened each day. Bruce had promised to bring her back to the village over the weekend to check on Rainie. She knew that both the child and her dog must be doing well because Ellis and Star had promised to get ahold of them if there were any issues with either. When Friday night finally came, Danielle wanted to go out on the town but Aedan and Nicole politely declined. Aedan hadn't told Nicole what he was planning but told her that they were going on a date in the evening and to wear something warm. He'd skipped out during lunch as well and refused to tell her what he was up to. She'd even quizzed Danielle asking if she knew what her twin was planning but even she didn't have a clue. They ate dinner inside and in relative quiet except for Neiko's snoring that could be heard from the living room. When dinner was over and the dishes done, Nicole waited to hear where they were going. Aedan instructed her to take Neiko out for a quick walk and when she returned, he would be ready for their date. Not quite sure what he was up to, she reluctantly did as he requested and headed out with her dog.

Once out of sight, Aedan set his plan into action. He strung up a few strands of dragonfly lights, lite several candles, quickly set up the projector that he'd borrowed from the library, popped the popcorn, opened the bottle of wine so it could breathe and set up the blankets and pillows on the air mattress that he'd borrowed from Danielle. He heard her before he saw her as she returned down the driveway and into their cabin. He met her with a dog treat for Neiko. When she informed her that she was ready to go, he held out a bandana.

"What?"

"Come here silly. This isn't for you to wear, well actually it is. It's to cover your eyes so I can show you your surprise."

"Surprise, I thought we were going out tonight on a date?" she asked, now totally confused.

"Trust me Nic. Let me cover your eyes and I'll show you your surprise in less than two minutes." She did as he said, and once her eyes were covered, he took her by the arm, holding her hand and slowly led her outside. Neiko stayed at her side as they made their way into the crisp fall night. She could smell the wood burning in the fire pit and smell the incense coming from the candles he had lit but nothing had prepared her for the setting he had created when she removed the bandana.

"What the hell?" she said, taking in the sights.

"Well, I thought we'd have movie night tonight if that's alright with you."

"Movie night? Outside? How?" she asked.

"You said that you love old fashioned movies, so I picked up a few at the library and thought it'd be fun to lay out under the stars and watch them. The greenhouse will make a perfect movie screen and I took the liberty of setting up a "bed" so to speak for us to lie on to watch whatever movie you'd like to start with. We have cheese and crackers, wine, a few other munchies and lots of blankets to snuggle under to keep warm."

Amazed by the thoughtfulness, Nicole stood silent, momentarily speechless. Their back yard had been turned into something out of a magazine. He'd strung light through the trees, had candles burning, a table set up with wine and beer, and had pulled just about every blanket they owned out onto an oversized air mattress, that Neiko was currently curled up on. In the thirty minutes that she'd been gone for her walk, he had created one of the most romantic vistas that she had ever seen, and he had done it all for her because she had simply stated that she liked old fashioned movies.

Aedan suddenly felt as if he'd done something wrong or crossed some forbidden line in the sand as she just stood there, not moving, not speaking. He quickly smiled and broke the silence.

"Hey, it was just a thought; probably a silly idea. And don't feel like you have to go freeze under the stars just to appease me. I can put everything away, it'll only take me a second," he said as he leaned over to start picking up. Quickly she grabbed his arm, and stopped him for moving. Standing just inches apart, she looked at the man who'd gone through so much trouble just to bring her joy and knew that she'd found her soulmate. Jared, her deceased husband had been her first love, her first everything and she would never forget him and he would always have a place in her heart. But Aedan was her present and her future and it took something so trivial as a picnic under the stars for her to realize what others had known all along. Here standing beside her was someone who loved her, genuinely loved her despite any baggage that she came with, despite her quirks and despite her reluctance to share her heart with anyone. Maria at the lodge had been right all along... sometimes people are given a second chance for love and she'd been one of the lucky ones who had. She wrapped her arms around her soldier, her lover, her friend and held on as if tomorrow wasn't a given.

Chapter 33

One of the benefits of living in the country was the amount of privacy and distance between neighbors; a fact that both Aedan and Nicole appreciated as they watched movie after movie well into the night. They laughed until they cried as they watched some black and white Charlie Chaplin films, snuggled during "When Harry Met Sally", and Nicole hid her eyes with the numerous blankets when they watched the 70's slicer film that Aedan had picked out, teasing her about all of the chick flicks he'd just endured. The wine and popcorn were long gone by the time they packed up the air mattress and bedding and called it a night. The night sky was illuminated with thousands of stars and there wasn't a cloud anywhere on the brisk fall night. The temperature was definitely reminding everyone that winter would be making her appearance sooner rather than later, a fact that was never forgotten when living in the North Country. Aedan had already made a mental note that he should bring in more wood to fill the basement to its capacity over the weekend.

Once in bed, they collapsed and slept; both in their own dream worlds and both without the demons that came to haunt them at night. With Aedan by her side, Nicole had finally come to terms with what had happened to her co-workers and knew that she was not to blame for the actions of the crazed gunmen who had murdered her friends. Finally opening up to someone, with that someone being Nicole who had essentially forced him to discuss what had happened in the dessert when he was serving; Aedan too was finally at peace with what he'd experienced while serving his country. Though he would never be able to completely forget; putting on a prosthetic every morning was a reminder of what the war had cost him, Aedan now was able to sleep most nights without the nightmares of war swirling in his head. And he had Nicole to thank for that.

The weekend flew by, and as the sun set behind the mountain range, Neiko jumped up and started barking long before Nicole realized what all the commotion was about. Aedan came up from the basement, where he'd spent most of the weekend stacking wood, and organizing the area that had once been a dedicated root cellar. Nicole had spent most of the weekend canning and cooking and now needed a place to store all of her efforts. As Aedan joined her, they went to the front door to see why her Shepherd was barking incessantly and were surprised to see two trucks coming down the drive. They immediately recognized Bruce's vehicle but had no idea who the owner of the vintage looking Chevy was. Both trucks came to a stop and almost immediately Sinjin jumped out and came bounding for the front door. Nicole instinctively opened her door, allowing Neiko freedom.

He immediately raced toward his canine friend and then toward Rainie who was exiting the rear of the truck and running toward him. Neiko, Sinjin and Rainie became one blur as they hugged, and rolled together in Nicole's front lawn, despite the frigid temperature. Nicole felt Aedan's arm go around her waist instinctively as they stood in their doorway watching not only his sister and Bruce approach but also Star and Ellis. Rainie's father appeared uncomfortable with his surroundings and for a moment Nicole was unsure if he'd make it to the cabin or retreat back to his truck.   But in the end, he squared his shoulders and as if taking a deep breath, forced himself forward.   Danny and Bruce entered their cabin with Danielle making herself at home as usual, while Bruce headed toward the kitchen and proceeded to pull out several beers from the frig. Aedan asked his sister what was going on but she ignored him.   Star made her approach toward Nicole while Ellis, though still slightly standoffish made his way toward Aedan who remained in close proximity to Nicole.   Stars said nothing but once close enough, embraced Nicole and held her tightly. Ellis walked directly to Aedan and once within striking distance, extended his hand.

"I was wrong. I was wrong about you, wrong about your woman; and wrong about a lot of things including the people of your community. And when I'm wrong I say I'm wrong.   You and your woman and your family are welcome in our home and in our community anytime. Remember that when you need a place to go," he added cryptically.

"Um, thank you Ellis," Nicole said, wanting to break up the serious energy that seemed to have enveloped the area.

"Please come inside. It's not much but at least it's a lot warmer than out here," she said, motioning for them to enter. She interrupted Rainie and the pups play, telling them to come inside as well whenever she was cold or tired. Once inside, all six crammed into the relatively compact confines of their tiny living room, each with drink in hand.

"So what do we owe this wonderful surprise?"

Star spoke first.

"Well, we know that you're going to say that you were just doing your job but that isn't 100% true. We know that what you did for our daughter went above and beyond your job and as my husband said, we will be forever grateful. And there's your dog," she continued, somewhat hesitantly. Before Star could continue, Nicole interrupted.

"Oh I'm sorry Star. It was an impulsive decision and offer. Has she been a nightmare; if so, I'm so sorry. I just really thought that the pup might be the catalyst for your daughter to push herself to get better. If she's been a burden, I can tell Rainie that Neiko misses his playmate and maybe Sinjin should stay with us. I didn't mean to do anything to make your life more difficult."

Danielle spoke up. "Nicole, zip it for a minute and let the woman speak," she said teasingly.

Star chuckled as she continued.

"As I was saying, your dog definitely has a lot of energy and doesn't always listen to commands, and we did catch her stealing food off of our countertop a few times; but, she has been the best thing to come into our lives, besides you and Aedan. Our little girl is beyond ecstatic and has come out of her shell so to speak. She has assumed all responsibility for that dog. She feeds her, walks her, picks up after her, brushes her and most importantly, loves that little mutt with every ounce of her heart. We came over to thank you for giving our daughter two precious gifts. You have her back her life with your medicine and you gave her a reason for living with your selfless gift."

Ellis finally spoke up for the first time since entering their home.

"What my wife is saying is that you gave to my daughter without expecting anything in return and she was essentially a stranger to you. You knew nothing about this area or our community yet you and the doctor moved here to help the people of the community, again, not expecting anything in return. Other than the doc's sister," Ellis continued as he looked directly at Aedan, "You have no one and no family here; no roots or ties to the land, yet you came."

He paused, as if still struggling with what he was to say next. "I speak for our town when I say that you and any of your blood are welcome in Destiny anytime and you are now part of our community." He then looked directed at Bruce. "The elders met yesterday and it was decided, unanimously I might add; that you my brother are still one of us and welcome as well. Maybe Nicole and Aedan opened up our very tightly closed eyes to the fact that our ways and beliefs are, and will always be, vital to the existence of our community; but, maybe it's time to reevaluate some of our customs. As your woman said, actually screamed at me," he said, winking at Danielle," sixteen is too young to make an absolute life changing decision. Please consider us your family again," he added, extending out his hand to his brother-in-law as Star watched on, not realizing that she was holding her breathe.

Bruce stood frozen, momentarily stunned by what he was hearing. But once it registered what was being offered to him again, it didn't take but a second to make his decision. Instead of taking his brother-in-laws hand, he grabbed him in a bear hug as laughter, clapping and crying all could be heard flowing from the cramped cabin.

Rainie and her two furry friends burst in the front door. "Brrrr momma, it's getting FREEZING out!" she explained as she ran to her mother's waiting arms.

"Well Miss Rainbow Elizabeth," Nicole said, as she stood up, "I might have just the trick to help warm you up. Come into the kitchen with me and let's make us some hot chocolate, how does that sound?"

"I don't know Nicki. I've never had it before. I don't think I've ever had cold chocolate either."

"Never had it huh? Well then Rainie, I think today is going to be your lucky day for every young lady like yourself needs to try hot chocolate with whipped cream on top. How does that sound?"

"Good I think. But do you have pretty sprinkles to put on top of the whipped topping" she asked shyly.

"I believe that I might just have a few sprinkles that I could spare," she said, as she put her arm around the shoulder of her pint sized friend as her two dogs sat patiently in the kitchen beside them, hoping for any handouts offered. Star and Danielle joined them in the kitchen so that the men could be alone and so that Danielle and Star could speak to Nicole out of earshot.

"Aedan told me that you've done a really great job canning and making preserves this weekend," Danielle said.

"That's a great start since the winters are pretty long up here and we don't get out quite as much as you would think. I'm not saying we're snowed in or cut off from civilization or anything like that; but, being self-sufficient and having a full pantry and root cellar going into the winter months up here is a matter of necessity. Moriah, Star, Miranda and a few of the other women always make a shopping trip this time of year into Errol and we were wondering if you'd like to join us; actually we're hoping you'll join us. We go next Saturday as it's their annual sidewalk and community garage sale. We make a day of it and usually bring two or three vehicles to carry all the provisions back with us that we purchase or barter for."

Slightly confused, Nicole quickly responded, "I absolutely love going to garage sales but what do you mean you barter? I don't think I understand. Where I come from, you go to sales, you find something you like and you pay for it, period. You do it differently up here?"

"Sort of, yes, sometimes we pay with cash but other times, we swap what we have for what they are selling.

Star makes the most amazing bracelets out of old tire spokes and Moriah is known county wide for her healing herbs and people not only trade whatever they're selling at their sales for her herbs but they pay her cash as well so for her it's always a win-win situation. As you've discovered, no one ventures over the river to their community so our biannual shopping trip is their only exposure to what Moriah has to offer and they look forward to us coming to their event almost as much as we look forward to going to it."

"Well that's all well and good but I don't have anything that I could barter with so I would love to join you but guess I'll have to pay with cold, hard cash," she laughed as she meticulously added the whipped cream on the top of Rainie's steaming cup of hot chocolate and before she handed it to the anxiously waiting child, she made sure she added a generous amount of sprinkles. Rainie's eyes grew bigger when she saw the steaming concoction coming her way.

"Be careful, it's very hot."

"Thanks Miss Nicole!"

"You're very welcome," she said, smiling down at the child. You're still taking the medicine that Doctor Aedan left for you right? You take them until they're completely gone, promise?"

"Ummm, this is really hot but REALLY good. Momma, can we get some of this for home," the child asked innocently.

"And yes Miss Nicole, momma makes me take them every morning and bedtime. I'm all better see," she said pulling up her pant leg.

Inspecting her wound which no longer needed a dressing and was nearly healed, Nicole smiled.

"I see. Keep up the good work," she said to both Star and her daughter.

Getting back to their topic of conversation, Danielle instructed Nicole to make some of her designer desserts that she'd listen to her brother brag about all summer. She instructed her to arrange them on cute little disposable plates in those glossy white wrappers that the high end shops use and then she promised to take care of the rest. Nicole didn't have much faith in selling or bartering her baked goods but agreed to give it a shot. Star and Danielle exchanged smiles knowing that Nicole's sweets would be a hit. They proceeded to explain what she could expect from their shopping trip. And whether she realized it or not, Danielle knew that Aedan might have something that she could use as barter as well.

Meanwhile, Bruce, Ellis and Aedan had other topics of conversation on their mind. Aedan had absolutely no idea what a tree cutting party was or consisted of, but was game to find out. Bruce omitted a few details so as to not totally freak his future brother-in-law out. He only told him that men from both sides of the river came together in the fall to harvest, hunt and prepare firewood for the following year. Knowing that he and Nicole could use more wood, he felt it only fair that he should offer his assistance if they were going to reap the benefits, and, explained that he knew how to use a chainsaw, but didn't own one. And didn't own a splitter either for that matter, but both Bruce and Ellis reassured him that he wouldn't need either. Bruce went on to explain that they would start their morning at sun up and that he should plan on it being a long day; hoping that Aedan's leg would be able to hold up. Ellis explained that it was customary for the men to spend the weekend in the woods while the women went to Errol on their annual shopping/stocking up spree. Aedan didn't understand the concept of garage sales at all. Bruce leaned in and simply told him that he would come to appreciate the weekend as it unfolded and that it was a must that he get a good night's sleep heading into the weekend. Bruce went on to say that after the woodcutting weekend, they moved right into hunting season with majority of the men of Mystique and Destiny coming together to hunt the various game in the area. Majority of the men in Ellis' community also hunted rabbit, bear, moose and turkey; but when deer season came around, they welcomed the men of Mystique to join them as there was always an overabundance of deer in the area and many hands tended to make light work, so to speak. Aedan was surprised to hear about the numerous ways that the women preserved the venison once the deer had been taken. He's never heard of canned venison before and had never personally dehydrated venison into jerky, no used the salt method, but was interested in learning. Both Bruce and Ellis explained that he'd have plenty of time to learn the numerous ways of preparing venison after hunting season started and even though the two communities kept to their own sides of the river, during hunting and harvesting season, they became one, and they weren't so diverse in their customs and beliefs after all.

Aedan was one to not make waves, so he was open to working with both communities as long as it didn't interfere with his time with Nicole. He had no one in his life other than his twin sister, and now Nicole. He also realized that she came from a big family, even if she had been adopted into the Flanahan family. He also realized that after meeting her family and especially her brother Jimmy and his lover, Gwen's best friend; that family was extremely important to the woman that he loved. Whether she realized it or not, once they settled in for the long winter that northern New Hampshire was known for, Nicole was going to start missing her extended family. And that was a fact that he'd have to discuss with her and also his sister and their co-workers at the clinic. She thought that they were settled in for the upcoming season but he knew better. Though he'd only known her for less than a year, he'd spent enough time with the woman to realize that her family was the most important thing in her life and even though she cared about him and loved her job as a nurse; she'd soon get lonesome for her siblings and parents. So sure he'd help get their cabin and the surrounding neighborhoods ready for the winter, but his first priority would be making sure that Nicole was happy and content. After living in a tent in the dessert, he knew that he could hang his hat anywhere as long as he had Nicole. But she needed more and he would not just settle anymore; her happiness was his mission. Ellis had alluded to the fact that there were many things that needed to be completed to survive in the North Country and that fall was the busy season for all of them. Living in a very compact cabin, Aedan knew that there was only so much that they could can, preserve and put in their already half full root cellar. He had yet to harvest their potatoes and the last of the tomatoes but felt confident that they had enough to tie them over. He didn't really understand the concept of being totally self-sufficient but was learning more and more every day and the more that he was around his sister and her fiancée, the more he began to realize just how very strong an independent his twin was. She ran her own business, was as capable

228

swinging an ax as she was sautéing something in a frying pan, and still remained gorgeous and confident stuck in dirt up to her elbows. It was no wonder that he was drawn to Nicole; it became very apparent to him that he was naturally drawn to independent strong women. Aedan momentarily thought back to their long deceased mother. She too had been a strong self-reliant woman. Thinking of her, he realized that she would have loved Nicole and probably would have loathed his ex-fiancée. He chuckled to himself, half listening to Ellis, as he thought of the woman that he'd given an engagement ring to. It now seemed like that relationship had been light years ago. How had he been so foolish back then to mistake complacency for love? They'd had absolutely nothing in common, including their goals, aspirations and interests and the only time that they truly were compatible was in bed. Thinking about it now, he realized that it had been the biggest mistake of his life and Moriah was right; everything happens for a reason and if that "mistake" hadn't happened, his path would never have led him to Nicole.

When the women, Rainie and the dogs rejoined them in the living room, Ellis took his cue and thanked them for the beer and stood to leave. Rainie already had Sinjin on a lease but when the pup pulled to attempt to go to Nicole, she felt her heart start to break for fear that the puppy was choosing Nicole over her. Nicole quickly saw the look on the child's face and reassured her that the puppy was just coming over to give kisses to Neiko. She excused herself momentarily and went back into the kitchen, only to return moments later with two rawhide bones, one for each dog. She handed the smaller bone to Rainie and explained that she was to allow the pup to chew on it for only 30 minutes per day; to which she quickly agreed. Once the three had left for their long ride back to Destiny, Bruce and Danielle also said their good-byes but not before Danny informed her brother that their present had made a huge impact on both communities and she wanted him to know how very proud she was to call him her brother. Hearing the sincerity in her voice not only made him smile, but hug her.

"I love you sis."

"I love you too Aedan and I'm so happy that you've found Nicole. But just remember," she whispered in his ear, "You can't marry her before Bruce and I get hitched!"

Pulling away, he started to say "I'm not" and was quickly cut off by his smiling sister.

"Good night Nic. Talk to you during the week and remember, bake some of those fancy Italian pastries to bring Saturday. Thanks for the beer. Good night y'all," she quickly said, making her departure, with her man in tow.

After they were all gone and the house was quiet again, Aedan asked her what the cookies were for and when Nicole explained, he wondered if there was any way to help her out. And then it dawned on him.

Chapter 34

It had felt great sleeping in their own bed she thought as she stretched slowly, trying not to disturb her man or her dog. Neiko had returned to sleeping in her bedroom now that his sidekick was no longer in the picture, or at least was temporarily gone. Nicole knew in her heart that she'd done the right thing and that Sinjin now belonged to a raven haired ten-year-old, but that didn't make her miss the pup any less. She'd healed and grown so much from the mangy, injured skeleton of a dog that they'd found trapped in a hunter's snare; and now was healthy, full of energy and occasionally, very rambunctious four legged terror on wheels. But when she looked at Rainie and Sinjin together, she knew that they were meant to be a team just like Neiko, her beloved Shepherd, was meant to be hers. As if he knew she was thinking about him, her dog got up from his position at the foot of the bed and came to her side. She rubbed his bed, and silently slipped out of bed. Looking back at the man still sleeping beside her, she felt such contentment and love. Here, in a little 1200 square foot cabin in the mountains of northern New Hampshire, she was finally home. She'd found a job that she was slowly beginning to really enjoy, was surrounded by honest, hardworking people who weren't superficial in any way, shape or form; and for the first time in her life, she was taking pride in learning new life skills and felt that she was doing her little part in making the planet more sustainable by going green. Yes, life had taken several unexpected turns for her during the last year but maybe, just maybe this is where she was supposed to be all along.

She was showered and dressed, with breakfast nearly finished when he joined her in their tiny kitchen. She greeted him with a quick kiss and a cup of steaming coffee. They had gotten into a comfortable rhythm and sharing close quarters was no longer a concern for either. Both were adjusting to their new lives and secretly, Aedan couldn't be happier. Once they both were ready, they locked up the cabin, a habit that Nicole still couldn't shake from all the years that she'd lived in the city. They then headed into Mystique for the start of their workweek.

Miranda appeared on edge as soon as they entered the kitchen which doubled as their break room. Not sure if maybe she was having yet another fight with her on again, off again boyfriend, Nicole said good morning but didn't inquire as to what was wrong. It only took a minute for Miranda to fill her on what was bothering her.

"Can you believe it? Oh my god, do you think that they actually have the technology to release an EMP?"

Somewhat confused about what she was fretting and rambling on about, Aedan tried to talk to the obviously upset woman currently standing in front of him. Before he could get a word in edgewise, she continued.

"My son is in the Middle East in the thick of that shit. What if this crap turns into a full blown war? WTF is going on with this world? Why can't people get along and why does everyone always hate the US so much," she asked as both Nicole and Aedan remained silent, not quite sure what to say.

Finally, Aedan spoke first, asking her what she was talking about that they'd obviously missed. He explained to her that they hadn't had the TV on, nor the radio for that matter and hadn't been on-line in days.

"You two really have no clue, do you?" she said, slight exasperated at their ignorance. I'm talking about the damn government of Alzotar threatening to declare war on us because of the president's push for the destruction of all of their nuclear weapons. Where the hell have you two been, under a rock or something? People have been talking about this for weeks now with that fucking czar or emperor or whatever the hell you call their leader over there in the dessert, threatening us. Our president keeps insisting that they don't have the manpower or the balls to attack the United States but from everything I've read about their technology, I think calling their bluff is a grave mistake. Some of the underground publications that I subscribe to all insist that he's wrong and that their government has provided documented proof that they not only have the means but have the technology to launch a full scale nuclear and/or biochemical war if they choose to. It terrifies me to think about what could happen if their threats come to fruition.

Aedan treaded gently.

"Miranda, many countries have threated us in the past, but no country has attacked the United States of America on our own land in any large scale attack since Pearl Harbor. Of course we've had terrorist attacks. But they were isolated incidents. 9/11 and the Boston Marathon bombing being prime examples. And although they were horrific, they were carried out by a few individuals, not an enemy nation. I'm not diminishing their importance; all I am saying is that they weren't full scale attacks and I don't think that there is a country with enough balls or technology for that matter, to wage a full scale attack on our land."

"God I hope you're right Aedan, I really do. But also, I hope that you heed my warning and stock up guys. We live differently up here than a lot of people in big cities, and while I know that we are a hardy lot and probably could survive a lot longer than city folk could; mark my words, that if our nation gets attacked, it won't be just the terrorists that we have to worry about. It'll be all the people that aren't nearly as prepared as we are up here in our little bum fuck town. Our country gets attacked, and suddenly there's no food or water or electricity or heat in the big cities, how do you think those people will react and where do you think they'll go? They'll go and do whatever they think they have to, to find food and services that they're lacking. I for one, am not sharing what I have stored and preserved and prepped. Just because someone else isn't prepared isn't my problem and whether you think I'm playing alarmist or not, I know that I would rather be prepared and not need to rely on everything that I've prepped for; than to have shit hit the fan and be in the same boat as all the other people who haven't stocked up on even the basics. Do you two," Miranda continued, somewhat sarcastically on her rant, "even have any idea what the most sought after items are, besides food and water?"

"Guns and ammo," both Nicole and Aedan replied in unison. Smiling at each other, they both added in rapid fire succession, allowing each other to take turns "Sources for cooking such as portable propane tanks, matches, alcohol to barter with, cigarettes to exchange for something you need, solar powered or wind up lamps for light, first aid supplies, overstock of an individual's prescription and non-prescription meds for generic ailments, wood for a heat source, iodine tablets for purifying drinking water or a water filtration system, some source of transportation such as a bicycle or horse."

As they kept going on and on listing the necessities for survival in the event of a biochemical attack, Miranda gained significantly more respect for her co-workers. Up until then, she had to admit to herself that she'd thought of them as a couple rich kids who showed up, at his sister's request, to play doctor and nurse in her cutesy little town; and after a stint, they'd go back to their fancy lives wherever that might be. She had never thought of them as grounded, wholesome or down to earth until that moment. Sure, she thought to herself, somewhat chastising herself now, they had dropped everything and raced into hostile territory, for lack of a better description of Destiny, to save the life of someone they didn't know or have any vested interest in. She'd given them a little credit for that; but still hadn't really considered them, someone like herself. But now, standing here, in their office's break room, looking at her co-workers, who were dressed as she was, in generic scrubs, sans fancy jewelry or flashy accessories, she realized how wrong she'd actually been in hastily judging them.

Miranda smiled as she ate crow but refused to acknowledge that she'd misjudged them, instead spinning the conversation back at them.

"Okay, so you know about majority of the essentials but have you stocked up on them? And how come you weren't aware of the threat from Alzotar? It's been all over the internet and the news channels for the last few days!"

"I, for one, rarely watch TV," Nicole was the first to respond. "And believe it or not, we're still trying to get everything organized and settled in before winter blows in. So I guess watching TV hasn't been my first priority, no offense," she added for good measure.

"None taken," Miranda responded back. Deanna, who'd walked in midway through the discussion at hand, finally spoke up. "Yeah, Miranda; not everyone sits on their fat ass watching CNN and the weather channel 24/7. Just because you're a news junkie doesn't mean all of us are!" she added, just to piss off her co-worker.

"Oh bite me Dee!"

"Would love to Miranda; but we've got a waiting room that's half full already so maybe we'd better get this show on the road and take care of them instead."

"Miranda," Aedan interrupted, ending the conversation. " would actually like to talk to you some more on preparedness because you sound very well educated on the subject, and I would appreciate any insight that you could give me. But for now, Deanna is right; we should probably get out there and help the people who need us."

Feeling a small victory and deciding that she liked the doc after all, she smiled and jumped out of her seat. "Deal. I'd be happy to sit and talk with you anytime about it. And I can show you the newsletters that I subscribe to that give me all sorts of helpful hints regarding self-sufficiency and preparedness for when the shit hits the fan."

Not wanting her to start again on any rants, he got out of his chair and headed toward the door.

"That would be great, thanks!"

Chapter 35

The week flew by with Aedan and Nicole busy every day at the clinic, seeing patients all day, with a multitude of ailments. Every evening proved just as busy as Nicole spent a few hours each night baking an assortment of treats to bring with her to the town wide sale on Saturday. Either she or Aedan, or sometimes both of them, took Neiko for a run before they ate supper; and then they both kept themselves busy doing different things. Most of the evenings, Aedan excused himself to go work out in the greenhouse but on the few occasions that she'd ventured out to offer him a beer or soda, it had taken her a minute or two to find him and when she did, he wasn't at all dirty like someone who was working with plants should be. She truly had no idea what he was up to but didn't worry about it either. She wasn't going to keep him on a short leash and at the end of the day, he was not obligated to tell her what he was doing anyway. They were sharing a cabin and working together, and yes, having wonderful sex on occasion, but that was it. She loved him but didn't think of them as a couple. He'd told her that he'd loved her a time or two but the times he'd made his proclamation, were in the heat of the moment types of events and she didn't really put much credence into how serious he'd been when he had offered those three special words. They were taking things day by day and not expecting anything from each other and that's the way they both had wanted it, right from the beginning.

Friday was finally winding down, and Nicole was getting nervous and excited about what she was bringing with her to the sales in the morning to barter with. He wanted to speak to Bruce in more detail to know what to expect during their tree cutting adventure in the morning anyway so he quickly agreed. Nicole told Aedan that she wanted to swing by their cabin first before heading over to Danielle and Bruce's to talk about the weekend. Once they were driving to their temporary home, she told Aedan just to drop her off and after she took care of her dog, she'd jog over to Danielle's to join them. He hesitated at first but then agreed, realizing that her absence would give him a brief interlude in which he could speak freely with both his sister and Bruce; a luxury that he hadn't had since hooking up with Nicole over the summer. He hadn't realized until then that his days, nights and life had revolved around the woman ever since he'd met her, and he and his sister really hadn't had any alone time in months. He'd had no one consistently in his life except for his twin sister since their parents died, and suddenly he realized just how much he'd missed their time together. She had been his best friend, confidant and rock while he served his country and was his coach and drill sergeant when he needed someone to force him to push himself beyond his limits after his injury. For almost as long as he could remember, it'd been just he and Danny against the world. Then Bruce entered the picture, and now Nicole; and nothing was the same anymore. He wasn't complaining whatsoever about the additions to his inner circle, because he now couldn't picture his life without her in it, and knew that his sister felt the same way about Bruce. It was just that the two of them had been each other's support system for so long that it was hard imagining anyone else could permeate his life so intensely and completely; but she had and he hadn't even realized it as it was happening right in front of his eyes.

He dropped her off at their cabin and quickly changed into jeans and an old t-shirt. Grabbing his ball cap that contrasted sharply with his summer bleached blonde hair, he shouted that he was heading over to his sister's and not to be too long playing with her pup since the sun was already starting to set. Nicole laughed as she played fetch with her shepherd who was momentarily distracted by Aedan's voice.

As Aedan pulled into his sister's drive, he immediately saw it and his only thought was "What the hell?" He hadn't put his truck into park before he was greeted by four smiling faces and a baby with curly auburn hair. It took just a second for it to synapse that here standing on his sister's porch were his love's favorite brother, her best friend and their baby. Everyone waved as he stepped out of the truck with a look of confusion in her face.

"Hey honey, heard there was a shopping trip going on this weekend," Gwen shouted to a bewildered Aedan. Jimmy approached Aedan, extending his hand to shake the man who stolen his kid sister's heart.

"How's it going? Hope you don't mind the invasion but when your sister and Gwen became friends on Facebook and started chatting, and then she heard there was some kind of community garage sale this weekend, I couldn't hold her back," he laughed.

"We were gonna stay in a hotel but your sister insisted we crash here. Bruce was just telling me about your project tomorrow. Guess it's a good thing I never wear anything too fancy cause I know how to swing an ax and use a chainsaw and told Bruce I'd love to give you a hand while my woman spends all my money," he joked.

Still a little speechless, he shook his future brother-in-law's hand.

"I have no idea what tomorrow is going to be like as I've never participated before, but another strong set of hands is always appreciated. Nic has no idea you're here does she?"

"Nope. Thought it'd be fun to surprise her," Danielle added.

"Oh boy, she is going to be surprised all right." Making eye contact with Gwen, he smiled.

"Well take a look at that little princess of yours. Hello Miss Lauren Rachel, you sure are a cute thing and it's very nice to meet you, again," he said as she took the rambunctious child from Gwen. He gave her a kiss and couldn't get over how big she'd gotten since the day he'd delivered her. That day and all the emotions it held came rushing back as he held the blue eyed, auburn haired princess in his arms. Nicole's brother Jimmy had been a basket case, Gwen had been a terrified mother to be, and Nicole had been a rock and his support system in delivering her best friend's child into this world. He'd never delivered a baby before, but with the support of his sister and Nicole, everything had gone off without a hitch. And here, holding the child he'd delivered brought back feelings that made him realize that regardless what path he and Nicole ended up on; they'd be forever tied together through the adventures and memories that they'd shared during the past year. As he held Gwen's child, he heard her before he saw her. Only his Nicole would be singing while she was running, he thought to himself. He waited until he saw her come around the bend and then freeze in her tracks the second she recognized the strange truck. It took her one split second to put two and two together and when she locked eyes with her favorite big brother and her best friend, she squealed and took off at a run towards her them. Jimmy stepped off Danny's porch and met his kid sister in the yard, grabbing her as she jumped into his arms and twirled her round and round. Everyone in attendance smiled, laughed and spilled a few tears seeing the love emitting from their reunion. Danielle knew the feeling because she felt it every time that she was reunited with Aedan after his deployment, and Bruce understood it since reuniting with his long lost sister Star, when she had started venturing across the river as an adult. Gwen didn't have any siblings but she had loved Nicole as her best friend for years, and Jimmy was the love of her life and the father of her child. Seeing them together and how happy it made them, in turn, made her happy. When Jimmy finally stopped twirling them before they both fell down or got sick from the vertigo, everyone joined them out on the lawn.

"Surprise," Gwen said as she hugged her best friend.

"You didn't honestly think that you and Danielle were going to go shopping all day and not include me, now did you? Miss Lauren needs to start young if she's going to be a professional shopper like myself, don't you think?" she kidded.

"Why didn't any of you tell me?" she said accusingly.

"It's not called a surprise if we had told you," Danielle said, hugging Nicole.

"And don't get mad at Aedan because he didn't know anything about it until he showed up here tonight. So now that you're here, let's get our asses inside and strategize with Gwen about our shopping attack tomorrow."

Arm in arm with Danielle and Gwen, Nicole walked toward the men waiting on the porch for their women.

The conversation flew from topic to topic and while the men's main focus of discussion was the tree cutting party that they were going to be part of in the morning. The women danced from subject to subject with Gwen asking a million questions and Danielle and Nicole attempting to answer all of them. They all laughed and cried, and had a wonderful time catching up. Nicole couldn't get over how great her best friend looked, especially after having a baby not that long ago. Love definitely looked good on both her friend Gwen and also her brother.

"So do you have all of your baking down for the sale tomorrow Nic?" Danielle asked.

Hesitant to commit, Nicole simply said, "I made a few things but I can't honestly see anyone trading tangible things just because they have a sweet tooth. I doubt any of them will even sell," she added.

"Well then it's a good thing that I brought a little something for us to barter with just in case your desserts are an epic fail," Gwen said confidently, pulling a huge bag out of her overstuffed diaper bag.

"What did you bring and how did you know to bring something?" Nicole asked suspiciously.

"I might have been in communication with her from time to time Nicole. It's all good and wait until you see what she brought! They're absolutely amazing!" Danielle responded.

"Um, yeah, about that," Gwen said as she started removing the contents of the large manila envelope.

"You know how I've always said that you're an amazing photographer?" she said hesitantly.

"Yes; but what has that got to do with anything?" Nicole asked, though she truly was afraid to ask.

"Well, I sort of took some of the pictures you've given me over the years and had them printed onto paper and then I made them into little notecards. See," she said, holding up a bundle of notecards that were neatly tied together with bailing twine, "I gave you credit for the pictures. See your name in the bottom right corner?" she added, trying to lessen the shock that Nicole's face was exhibiting at that very moment.

"You are just an amazing photographer and I thought why not share some of that beauty with others, especially if you're bartering with the notecards not selling them per say. Say you're not mad Nic," she almost pleaded, when her best friend still remained silent.

Taking them from Gwen's outstretched hand, Nicole stared down at what Gwen had created with her pictures. She didn't know what to say when she looked at the various prints, each bringing back wonderful memories of when and where they were shot. And then it dawned on her; each and every one of them had been taken since Aedan had entered her life. Gwen had used her favorite shot of the Bull Moose that Aedan had pointed out to her as they were entering the Lodge in Maine. She had taken her favorite shot looking down a train track and matted in on a soft rust colored paper, the picture of a sunset on a coral colored paper, her favorite mountain view on another and lastly, the lucky shots she managed to capture of the hawk that kept returning to the lodge on another. Altogether, she'd used eight of Nicole's favorite shots and captured their essence with the colored paper she'd had them printed on. As she viewed the various prints, she couldn't help it, the tears started flowing. Seeing her start to cry, Gwen attempted to put the pictures back in the envelope that she was still holding.

"It's okay Nic if you don't like them. I thought it was just a thought but if you don't like them or want me to use them, I can put them right back. Not a big deal."

"Not like them? Oh my god," she said as she wiped the tears from her eyes. "They are amazing! You took my mediocre pictures and made them look amazing.

"And cheap since I know the owner of the print shop," Gwen added, now that she could relax after realizing that her best friend loved her idea. "I bet they'll be awesome for bartering or getting outright cash for."

"So how exactly does this village wide sale work Danielle," Gwen asked as Nicole continued to stare at her prints.

"And I brought a few little trinkets that Jimmy and I have started making and selling." She pulled out a handful of tiny baggies with the most unique earrings that either Danielle or Nicole had seen in a long time. Made of recycled glass and metal, Gwen held them up to catch the waning sunlight. Each was unique and whimsical, and absolutely beautiful.

"Wow! Let me take a look at those," Danielle stated as she grabbed the bag from Gwen's hand. "What are you getting for a pair? And how much are you charging for shipping?" As she was finishing her questions, Aedan walked in, carrying a small tote bag. He knew by the look on his sister's face that the wheels in that business minded head of hers were hard at work and turning quickly. That's one thing that he could say for his sister, she had an uncanny business sense and always knew a good idea when he saw it. When Gwen hesitantly responded what she and Jimmy were selling the earrings for at craft fairs and farmer's markets; she looked at her friend in disbelief.

"Would you like to be making triple that per pair? I happen to dabble quite a bit with online sales and have a website that generates several hits per day and at least a few sales per day. If you're interested, I'd be more than willing to work something out with you that benefits us both and I could showcase your earrings, and your prints Nicole," she said, looking back Nicole's way.

Aedan leaned in toward Jimmy, who had now joined them in the kitchen and whispered.

"Don't let her fool you, Danny gets several hundred hits in any given week and sometimes can hardly keep up with the demand for her stained glass pieces. Your earrings would sell very quickly on her website."

Jimmy looked at him in almost disbelief. They had been trying so hard to come up with ways to supplement their income and still allow Gwen to remain at home with their baby. If what Aedan and Danielle were saying was true, this might just be the answer to their prayers. Gwen looked over at her love and seeing the huge grin coming over his face, she turned toward Danielle and responded.

"I think they're pretty, but let's see how they sell or if anyone is interested in trading what they have for them, and if they are; then we'll definitely talk ok?" she answered, not wanting to get too excited or her hopes up too high.

"I have posted some of them on Facebook with many of my friends ordering them, but honestly, I thought they were just being nice to humor me."

"I would like to purchase this pair Gwen," Aedan said as he held up a pair of earrings that were almost an exact shade of the color of Nicole's eyes. The green in the glass was between a moss green a deep forest green and he knew that they'd look stunning on her. Before Gwen, who was always loquacious could even say a word, he opened up his wallet and handed her a fifty.

Dumbfounded, she looked at him and finally responded.

"My purse is still in the truck Aedan, so give me a second to go get you change."

"What do I need change for? Danny said you should be charging 3x what you were, so that comes to $45 and I figure by the time you add tax on, $50's about right. And no," he joked, "I'm not paying you shipping and handling since you're in the same room as I am and you handed them to me," he joked.

"You mean to tell me you'd pay $50 for one pair of earrings? You'd really not hesitate, look at them and think they're worth $50?"

"Um... I think I just did. Don't sell yourself short Gwen. You and Jimmy put a lot of time working the wire around the glass, rubbing down the rough edges and should be charging a lot more than you were. You have to pay yourself for the time and effort it takes to make each one by hand; so yes, I think they are most definitely worth $50. And when I give them to that beautiful woman standing across the room," he said as he smiled at Nicole, "I might very well get lucky tonight," he said as he winked at her.

Elbowing him, Jimmy reminded him that the woman he hoped to get lucky with was still his kid sister and he'd really prefer to not have that type of information. Everyone got a good chuckle and continued looking at the vast assortment of earrings that they'd created. Danielle had stepped out of the room momentarily and when she reappeared, she was grinning ear to ear and had Bruce with her. Knowing his sister, the way he did, Aedan knew immediately that she was up to something.

"What'd you do Danny?"

"Oh nothing, besides Aedan," diverting the attention from herself, "don't you have something in that bag you're holding that you'd like to show Nicole and the rest of us?"

Now the center of attention, he felt very uncomfortable.

"No, it can wait," he responded quickly, which only stimulated more interest in whatever was in the canvas bag clutched under his arm. Nicole made her way across the room and kidded, "Whatcha got in there Aedan? Something for me, so you can get lucky as you put it," she teased.

"Oh my ears," Jimmy added, pretending to be offended as he lifted his hands to his head.

"Honest, it's nothing Nic. I just grabbed a few things that I thought you might be able to barter with. They probably won't be anything anyone is interested in, but I figured, what the heck, why not try." Reluctantly, he lifted out the contents of the bag and Nicole gasped as she saw them.

"Where did you get those?" she asked as she looked at the prints he was holding.

"I sort of dabble with paint and sometimes charcoal," he responded hesitantly.

Almost immediately, her eyes lifted to the massive print above Danielle's fireplace mantel. "Oh my God, you painted that didn't you?" she asked, half accusing, but already knowing the answer.

"Guilty. I have always loved to paint; and when you're limited in your walking ability after your leg is blown off, you have plenty of time to work on honing your technique. It's just something that brings me peace, much like playing guitar provides you solace."

"I think you're amazing Aedan," she said as she threw herself into his arms. "Absolutely amazing!"

"Oh Christ, they're gonna go at it right here in your living room Bruce. Jesus Christ," her brother kidded, completely in jest. Gwen and Danielle took a look at the prints that Nicole had in her grasp and both nodded in approval.

"You know Aedan, you've fought me for so long about showcasing your artwork. I honestly think you should consider letting me print them out and sell your prints. You're more talented than you give yourself credit for. Between Gwen's jewelry and notecards, I'm already going to have to redesign my website. So why not let me mass produce your artwork and Nicole's pictures as well. If they sell, they sell and if not, nothing's lost. So what do you think? Are you two both willing to at least let me give it a shot?" she asked, knowing that she had them cornered and they'd have no choice but to consent.

"The fear of rejection terrifies me Danielle, and the thought that maybe not even one of my prints will sell is very scary," Nicole said carefully. "But I'm willing to give it a shot if you are Aedan," she interjected, knowing that she was leaving the final decision entirely in his hands.

"So what do you say Aedan," his sister said, taking advantage of the moment, "Are you going to let me make you a very rich man?" she kidded.

"Money doesn't buy you happiness or love Danielle, and I already have plenty of both. But if Nicole is willing to sell her artwork, so am I; but mine is under one condition."

"And what might that be dear brother of mine?" she asked tentatively.

"You can mass produce anything that I have, as long 75% of the profit from the sales is donated back to the Wounded Warrior Project that Maria and Alfred have set up at the Lodge. And it has to be donated to them anonymously. Alfred is never to learn that I have anything to do with the donation, okay?" Knowing it was futile to argue with her brother, she leaned in and gave him a kiss on the cheek. "Deal."

"That is an awesome idea Aedan! But I'm not quite as generous as you. I will donate 30 percent of all of my sales also Danielle, with the remaining 70% to be put into a college trust fund for my nieces and nephews."

"That's very generous Nic," Jimmy spoke up. "But if you're going through the effort of setting up trust funds for your nieces and nephews, don't you think it would make sense to set up a trust fund for your children as well?" he asked innocently.

"Last I knew," she responded in an almost near whisper, I don't have any children and don't anticipate having any anytime soon either."

Danielle could tell by her expression, that it was a very painful subject for the woman who'd become a dear friend to her.

"I think your brother is right. You never know what fate has in store for you, so I'd set up that trust fund for all of your brother's children; but also, set some aside for the future, should you choose to have children someday."

Wanting the discussion to come to an end, Gwen interjected. "This has been an amazing evening, but since shopping and spending money has a tendency to exhaust me, I think I'll say my good night's and call it a night. But before I retire for the evening, Danielle, what was the surprise you said you were going to tell us?"

"Well, I made a few calls and was able to secure us a table for tomorrow's event in town. All of your stuff, including Aedan's prints will be for sale tomorrow during The town's Pioneer Weekend! I bribed one of the teenagers whom I know has been saving her money to purchase one of my stained glass wind chimes. Told her it's hers free if she'll man the table while we're shopping tomorrow. Pretty ingenious, don't you think?"

"Sure," Nicole said, still not completely convinced that anyone would want her prints, "if you think so. Guess tomorrow will be sort of a trial run to see if anyone has any value in our artwork," she laughed. She leaned on to touch her now sleeping god child and both she and Aedan said their good nights as well. Nicole reminded Bruce and Jimmy that she'd have breakfast waiting for them at 7am and that they'd better be on time so as to not screw up their shopping adventure. Danielle and Gwen reassured her that their men would not be late and that they'd be over by 7:30 for round two of whatever breakfast entrees she was whipping up.

Chapter 36

Bruce and Jimmy entered her cabin at precisely 6:59am to the smell of bacon, waffles, sausage, and coffee. They were greeted by Aedan and Neiko, and found Nicole working her magic creating a marvelous looking western omelet. She had pulled out and cleaned an antique looking thermos to take some of the coffee she'd brewed for them into the woods. Bruce chuckled and tried to explain that the beverages that they'd be consuming would be a little stronger than coffee. Jimmy, a recovering alcoholic got his drift and told his sister that he'd love to bring the thermos with him, along with a bottle or two of water. He'd remained sober for a few years now and wasn't about to do anything to jeopardize his life and the life he'd made with Gwen. Once the food was ready, all three men dug in and ate like it was their last meal. They made small talk and were completely stuffed about the time that Danielle and Gwen, along with little Lauren entered the cabin. Just prior to departing, Aedan pulled Nicole aside and kissed her for no reason, other than she was there and he was leaving. She had never quite understood what it was about that man, his simple kiss sent shock waves down her spine. The three of them all promised to be safe and back before dark and the women said their goodbyes simultaneously. Once they were alone, they sat down to their meal and finalized their shopping strategy.

They took Danielle's truck after loading up their wares, and installing Lauren's car seat and headed towards their destination in town. Danielle explained the history of the town and how the weekend had come to be known as Pioneer Days as they made their way over to the girl's home who would be manning their table during the sale. They greeted her and then made their way towards Errol. Once in town, they assisted Samantha in the setting up of the table and their products and when everything was organized, they set off to check out the sales.

The men made their way to Destiny with Bruce driving. Once parked on the outskirts of town, they exited the truck to the sound of a multitude of chainsaws. Jimmy's first impression was that he'd stepped back in time or had entered the twilight zone when he looked around at the primitive environment unfolding in front of him. He saw men and their teams of horses dragging massive logs, men using both chainsaws and handsaws and to his left, he watched as a team of men winched a massive maple over onto its side with some type of hand controlled winch. His first thought was that many of the men in attendance looked to be Native American but quickly realized that they weren't. It was just that many of the men hard at work had very distinctive features, and others like Aedan, were polar opposites with his blonde hair and blue eyes. As they made their way closer, Jimmy looked into the eyes of Star's husband and thought the man was looking right through him; and his first impression of the menacing looking Neanderthal looking man was not impressive. He felt instant dislike for the man, but wasn't sure why.

Bruce made his introductions of the men who'd stopped work long enough to greet them and then asked where they were to start. Ellis continued to study Jimmy as Bruce talked; when he finally approached him, putting Jimmy on edge.

"Your sister saved my daughter's life. And I will be forever indebted to her. So we are family," he said as he extended his hand, with Jimmy reluctantly shaking it. "When the time comes, know that you and your woman are welcome here. You are her favorite and the one she counts on most, so do not ever let her down."

Totally perplexed by the man's words, Jimmy responded.

"I'm not quite sure how or when my kid sister saved your little girl's life; but she was probably doing what she does best. She has been healing and helping people since we were kids, and I'm glad that she was able to help your daughter. =ut you don't owe her or me anything. And I'm not quite sure what time you're talking about coming. I'm only up here for a few days so my woman could visit her best friend and I could help you out with your wood."

"You'll know soon enough," was Ellis' only response as he pointed to where the men would be most useful. Bruce, Aedan and a very confused Jimmy made their way to the group of men that Ellis had pointed at and started in loading wood into an oversized splitter. As they worked in silence, Jimmy couldn't get what Ellis had said out of his mind. Finally, needing to break the ice, he said, "Gwen and I are planning on getting married in the spring at Nicole's home on Sycamore Lane. We've been discussing it and we love the place so much that we can't think of anywhere else where we'd like to become man and wife, and we would very much like it if you both could make it to our wedding. Of course, she'll send y'all the formal invitations and such, but I know it's really important to have her friends and family present, so I hope you'll set the date aside."

"That's great Jimmy. I bet you haven't told Nicole yet have you? Cause if you had, she would have been stoning me already with a million ideas that she'd have on how the place should be decorated!" he teased.

"Nope, I figured I'd take care of telling you guys and she could take care of telling the women. Did you and Danielle set a date yet?" he asked Bruce.

"Actually, he said, looking over at his future brother-in-law, "we did. We're getting hitched in six weeks, and I was sort of hoping Aedan, that you'd be my best man. I don't have a father who's living and he wouldn't have been able to stand up for me even if he were still alive. I think of you as a brother, so it would only make sense to ask you. What do you say?"

"If you're finally going to make an honest woman out of my sister, then the answer is a resounding yes. Yes, I will stand up in your wedding, and yes, I will be your best man!"

By midday, the three women's arms were loaded down with wares and goods that they had purchased at various stores and from various vendors. As they made their way back to Danielle's truck to unload everything, they passed Samantha who was curled up with a book and her feet up on the table that they'd brought. Not quite sure what was going on, Nicole approached the girl asking her where all of their products were. Smiling but not saying a word, she reached into her purse and withdrew three different stacks of bills, each secured lightly with paper clips. Mesmerized, Gwen looked at Nicole and then at Danielle for answers.

Everything sold already," Danielle asked, surprising even herself.

"Everything's been sold for over an hour now," the young girl responded. I think you must have underpriced everything because everyone went nuts over everything.

I had to keep passing out business cards for your website Danielle because people must be telling people and women kept stopping here asking for more stuff. I didn't know what to do so I directed them to your website. I hope that was alright?"

"That is more than alright Samantha. And you did a great job!"

"Um, if you don't have any more for me to sell for you, can I leave? My cousin is here and about to head back to Mystique so I can catch a ride with her if that's okay with you."

"Yeah, sure. Thanks again Sam for helping us out on such short notice. Swing by the house tomorrow and I'll give you the wind chime okay?"

"K, thanks Danny."

As Danielle started to fold up the table that they'd used for the sale, she looked at Nicole and Gwen who'd remained pretty much speechless since seeing their products had all sold. Danielle's smirk was absolutely an "I told you so look" and both of them knew it. Once Danielle had the table and their purchases loaded into her truck and was ready for round two of shopping, she turned towards her companions. "Well, was I right or was I right?" she asked smugly. "And did you count your profit yet ladies? That's the fun part."

"I still can't believe that people paid the prices that I had put on the earrings. I thought selling them for $15 was okay since we made roughly $13 on each pair. And honestly, I thought marking them up to $29.99 for a flea market was ludicrous but I admit Danielle, you were right."

"Just wait until we're selling them at $49.99 on line and they're still selling like hot cakes," Danielle couldn't help but add. "And you," she said, looking at Nicole, "You didn't believe me either but I knew that your notecards and your prints, and your homemade pastries would sell. And it was ingenious adding the cute little recipe cards that you typed up and included with the food. People probably bought them because you offered them the recipe and they think that they can replicate them at home. Very business savvy Ms. Brentwood, very savvy!"

"I noticed that your stained glass mirror and sun-catchers and even your gazing ball are also sold Danielle so you must be very happy."

"I am. The few items that I brought were sort of on-line rejects so to speak. I'd had them showcased for months now and they hadn't sold; so I reduced their prices by only 15% and ta da, they sold here. Of course, not having to pay shipping doesn't hurt either."

Before they started out again, both Nicole and Gwen counted their earnings and were shocked when they realized how much they'd made. Then the three of them set off toward the other side streets that they hadn't hit yet as Lauren Rachel slept soundly in her stroller. They continued shopping all day, finding great deals everywhere and when completed shopped out, they loaded up and headed for Mystique River. As they made their way down the road, Gwen who wasn't known for keeping a secret, started talking; making generalizations at first.

"Hey Nicole, do you ever wonder about your birthparents? I know that's sort of a weird, out of the ordinary question but now that I'm a mother and all, I can't imagine my life without my daughter and suffice it to say, I think about her almost every moment of every day. Don't get me wrong, I love your brother to pieces, but there's something about the bond between a mother and her daughter. All's I'm getting at is that I'm sure your birth mother, even though she had to give you up, still thinks about you all the time as well."

Nicole didn't answer immediately, but when she did, it was an honest answer.

"I think about her sometimes and have dreams about both of them sometimes but it doesn't consume me. She had her reasons for doing what she did and who am I to judge her? I wish I knew who I looked like though and I guess that sure, maybe I'd like to sit down and talk with her one time; but that's about it. I know who I am and what I am. I have the parents who raised me to thank for that. Genetics determined my eye color, and hair color, but the person I am today was not predetermined when an egg and sperm did the tango. I have two incredible people that I call mom and dad to take credit for that."

"That is a pretty amazing outlook Nicole," Danielle said, choosing her words carefully.

"And I'm sure if your mother had been pregnant with you in current times, not thirty years ago, her decision might have been different. Sometimes, it's not just family pressures, but societal pressures as well that force people to make decisions that they otherwise wouldn't make. Regardless, we're glad that your path led you to us, and the more time I spend with you Ms. Brentwood," she kidded, "the more I understand why my brother is so head over heels in love with you."

"What are you talking about Danny? Your brother likes my cooking and sex; and that's about it. We spent a summer together and now are dancing our way through working together but neither of us said anything about being in love."

"And if you actually believe that, then I'm very disappointed in you, and my brother for that matter. Anyone just has to look at you two to know you're in love, and if my brother hasn't admitted that fact to you yet, then he's as blind as you appear to be."

Knowing that a change of subject was crucial; Gwen interrupted as they pulled into Danielle's drive. "Her name is Arla."

Both Danielle and Nicole spoke simultaneously, with both of their voices slightly on edge. "Whose name is Arla?"

Before straight out answering the women that Gwen knew both had tempers, she circled around the question. "You know I've cut down my real estate schedule tremendously so I can be home with my princess," she said, gazing at her sleeping child.

"Well, it leaves me plenty of time to play around on the computer when she's sleeping. I sort of got intrigued with sites that trace a family's lineage after having my daughter and one site lead to another and another and next thing you know, I was on various adoption sites and birthmother's searching for their birth children that they gave up."

Nicole felt the hair starting to stand up on the back of her neck as Gwen continued. "Spit it out Gwen," she all but demanded.

"Okay, here goes. I stumbled upon a site where birth mothers provide dates of birth, place of birth etc., and any other identifying information that they have about the child that they gave up. It's sort of like a registry. And there was one posting that matches you Nicole. The woman is searching for her daughter, born on your date and in the hospital where you were born; and if she is truly your mother, well, her name is Arla. And I don't know anymore but I think that she has a beautiful name and if she's searching for you, then she can't be all bad right?" she asked, hoping that she hadn't stepped over the line of friendship.

Now both Danielle and Nicole had goosebumps but only Nicole spoke. It might just be a coincidence Gwen. And no, no I'm not upset that you did the research that you did. Does Jimmy know what you discovered? I really don't want this information getting back to my parents because as far as I'm concerned, they are my parents and no one will ever take their place in my heart."

It was Danielle's time to add something to the conversation and she treaded lightly as she said it.

"Nic, sometimes a birthparent searches for their child solely to make sure that they turned out alright and are happy. Sometimes they need that to lessen the guilt that they have for abandoning the child in the first place and sights like the one Gwen found, serve that purpose. They aren't meant to replace one parent with another. It's none of my business, but all I'm saying is keep that in mind if you choose to do anything with the information that Gwen has uncovered."

Nicole remained silent, lost in her thoughts as they exited the truck. There were no trucks in the drive and it was apparent by the silence that the men must be still working in Destiny, or back along the river in town. Nicole excused herself momentarily, stating that she'd run over to her cabin to let Neiko outside, and then come right back. Both Gwen and Danielle offered to go with her, which she politely declined either of their offers because she really needed a few minutes alone to digest what Gwen had told her. Both women had half expected that she would respond that way, and both hoped that the information hadn't spoiled what had otherwise been a perfect day. As Nicole truckk drove down the driveway, Danielle immediately cornered Gwen.

"Quick, before Nicole gets back; answer me one quick question, does that site have pictures by any chance?"

Not sure why she was asking, Gwen reluctantly responded, "Yes, everyone who's looking for someone usually has at least one picture of themselves or one of who they're looking for. Why?"

"I'd really prefer to not divulge why quite yet because it's a long shot; but can you possibly pull up the picture of Nicole's birth mother quickly before she comes back? I really need to see the picture of the woman who gave birth to her."

Having no idea why it mattered to her, but by her persistence, Gwen could tell that it did, she started up her laptop and pulled up the site. It only took a one second glance at the screen for Danielle to be sure and by the way she gasped, Gwen knew that somehow, some way her new friend knew her best friend's birthmother. Before she could ask what the connection was, they heard Nicole's truck coming back down the drive. Gwen quickly shut off the computer and both women sat down with wine glasses in hand, trying to look casual and relaxed. Nicole entered the home and was handed a glass by Gwen who had already filled it, adding ice like she knew Nicole always drank it.

"Neiko alright when you got home?" Danielle asked casually.

"Yeah, he's never a problem. Oh, I forgot to ask you, when you saw Star and Moriah and the othe's from Destiny earlier today; did they say when they were coming over to finish harvesting the last of the vegetables in the greenhouse?"

"Actually, it's funny you should mention it because they said that they'd come over tomorrow morning early if it's alright with you and Aedan. Star said that the men would most likely still be cutting the wood most of tomorrow so if the timing works for you, then it's perfect for them.

"Sure," Nicole said. "And what if we tell the men and women who come over to all plan on staying for a cookout and maybe a bonfire afterward? You know it's just as easy to cook for six as it is for twenty," she added. "And after cooking for a gang all summer, I've become accustomed with cooking for large crowds!"

Thinking that it was merely a coincidence that Nicole was handing her the opportunity that she'd been looking for, Danielle seized the moment and told her that it sounded like a great idea. With the first bottle of wine suddenly empty, the three filled their glasses again once Danielle opened a much larger second bottle. Laughter could be heard practically across the river as the three women laughed and exchanged stories about their best bargains of the day, they and about the antics that Nicole and Gwen used to get into. Danielle opened up a little about she and her brother's childhood and how hard it had been when they'd lost their parents when they were only teenagers. Gwen took the opportunity to reassure Nicole that her brother had never touched another drop of alcohol since they'd been together, a fact that Nicole would be forever grateful for her friend giving him a second chance and new lease on life and love. After they all had consumed far more alcohol than they should have, Danielle asked Nicole the question that she'd wanted to ask her from the day they'd met.

"I know you care a lot about my brother whether you'll admit it or not; but I need to know, does it matter to you that he's missing half his leg? Even though he can do most things that any man can, he will always have a few limitations because of the prosthetic. Does that bother you?" she asked.

Choosing her words carefully, Nicole smiled.

"Danielle, I know that you've had to be your brother's protector, surrogate mother so to speak, and his best friend for a very long time. And I will never challenge the bond that you as twins must have, nor would I want to attempt to challenge that bond. But before I answer that question, I have one for you," she said, still smiling. "Where did I first meet you and your brother?"

"That's silly Nic; we met on top of St. Regis Mountain, back in Paul Smith's, why?"

"That's correct. We met on top of a mountain, after each of us had climbed over three miles to get to the summit. We climbed through creek beds, over tree stumps, rocks and boulders, correct?"

"Correct. But what has that got to do with anything?" Danielle asked, somewhat confused.

Not letting her off the hook quite yet, Nicole continued. And after that, wasn't Aedan hitchhiking from New Hampshire to Maine, walking while carrying a huge backpack? And after we met for the second time, didn't he go running with me, ride horseback with me, hike with me, and eventually do the horizontal tango with me?"

Finally seeing where Nicole's train of thought was going, Danielle smiled back at the women who'd stolen her brother's heart. She too, had grown to love Nicole and was so happy that she saw her brother as a whole man, not just an injured ex-soldier.

"You really aren't affected by his injury are you?"

"Nope, your brother is a pain in the ass and can be very bossy at times, very stubborn at times, and is definitely hardheaded all of the time. But he's wore me down and I've sort of come to love the guy. And the way I was brought up, if you love someone, you love the entire person, limitations and all."

Gwen and Danielle looked at each other and silently gave each other high five's. It took Nicole a few seconds to realize what she'd just said.

"Oh my God," she thought to herself, "I just admitted out loud that I love her brother." Realizing that she was now the absolute center of attention, she looked at the two women closest to her heart and smiled. "I really just said I love Aedan didn't I?"

"Yup," they both simultaneously responded; and the three of them clanked their wine glasses together.

Chapter 37

It was practically dark. The food was cold and the women were drunk when Bruce, Jimmy and Aedan made their way inside. All came to the same conclusion once they saw the empty wine bottles, and the half empty bottle of Tequila. The women were chilling on the sofa and loveseat, while Jimmy's daughter slept soundly in the spare bedroom, unaware of the drunken mess her mother was, at the moment. Instead of creating any type of scene, or getting upset with something that was already done; they simply went to their respective women and greeted them with kisses and hugs and a few shaking of heads. The women giggled, and laughed, but made no apologies or stories regarding how they had gotten in their current predicament. When asked how they made out with their wares at the festival, each pulled out a wad of money and showed their men.

"Every sticking thing sold! Cannot believe that people actually paid that kind of money for one of my prints, let alone the simplistic desserts that I made, but they did! They actually bought them all. I wouldn't believe it if I didn't have the cash to prove it!"

"Told you you're a very talented photographer Nic," Aedan said as he subconsciously rubbed her back, a move that didn't go unnoticed by his twin.

Jimmy looked at Gwen, asking her how she did. She handed him the pile of money with him noting $20's and 50's mixed in a few $10's and only a few smaller bills. "Danielle insisted that we price the earrings much higher than I thought we should; and every pair sold Jimmy, every last pair! I can't freaking believe it. I really can't!" she exclaimed.

"I knew they were pretty and unique but maybe we're really onto something Jimmy! Maybe this is a fresh start for us and I'm so incredibly happy that we made the trip up here. Everything about this area is so wonderful. As much as I love Nicole's home, I could move up here in a heartbeat. There's something about small towns that is so welcoming. I met so many nice people today and everyone was so nice, making a fuss over our girl and everyone is so talkative. Strangers actually talk to one another around here; it's wild," she said as she practically fell over on the couch.

"I think it's time to get this one to bed," he said as he laughed at this fiancée's lack of coordination. Aedan took his cue and put his hand out for Nicole. "Think we should take our money and run as well. What do you say Nic?" She grabbed his hand and let him pull her to a standing position. "What's this "our" money shit?" she kidded as he held her tight.

"How about I just let you take me home okay?" she said, winking at him. "Works for me," he said as they made their way toward the door.

"Oh, wait! I cooked your supper honey. I put it on a plate for you and everything," she said as she tried to pull away from him. Before she could get away, Bruce handed her the plate in question and knew it was meant for him by the cute hearts Nicole had drawn on the foil covering it.

"Yup, I had better marry my woman before Aedan and Nicole tie the knot or I'll never hear the end of it," he thought to himself as he handed Aedan the plate of food. As they were about to leave, Danielle shouted a reminder to Nicole that everyone would be over to work in the greenhouse at sun up or close to it. At the moment, it didn't seem like a big deal but Aedan wondered what her head would feel like in the morning.

Danielle and Bruce finished picking up the kitchen and made their way to bed as well. There were a few things that she wanted to tell him about but once her head hit the pillow, she was out. Whatever it was that she had on her mind would have to wait until tomorrow night he thought to himself as he slipped in beside her.

Chapter 38

Their men took off before sun up, with Bruce honking the horn on his truck as he waited for Aedan to emerge from his cabin. Nicole had been sleeping soundly until she heard the blast, which caused her to bolt from the bed. It was definitely not the smartest move when nursing a hangover, especially the size of the one that she currently had. Aedan must have expected it because when she made her way into the bathroom, she found a glass of water and Extra Strength Tylenol sitting on the vanity. Once done in the bathroom, she made her way toward the kitchen to let Neiko outside. It was on the kitchen table that she found a note.

Hey baby:

I took care of your pup for you so don't worry about him. Your tea is in the microwave; I know, we shouldn't use the extra electricity but I figured you'd need a cup post haste and it sometimes takes forever on the stovetop to heat so indulge yourself my love. Must have been one hell of an evening from the empty wine bottles that were scattered about; sorry Bruce, Jimmy and I had to miss it.

The more time that I spend with your brother, the more I like him. He really is a good guy Nicole and he absolutely loves you to pieces. I know he's had demons in the past, who hasn't; but he's straightened out his life and wants nothing more than to be a good father to his daughter, and good provider and husband to Gwen. I'm so glad that he's accepted me for who I am as well.

My sister said something about you inviting everyone over for a massive cook out this evening after we're done with the wood. If you don't want to extend that invitation any longer (in light of the way I know you must be feeling right about now), don't worry about it. I'm sure we can get everyone together another time. For now, make sure you hydrate and not work too hard in the garden and greenhouse today. I'll see you later this afternoon okay? Remember, hydrate, hydrate, hydrate!

Love you Nicole Rose...

Aedan

Nicole read and reread the note that he'd left for her, next to a plate with two huge donuts on it. How was it that she'd been so lucky all her life, she now wondered? She grew up in a home full of love, had wonderful friends that she'd had all her life and was still in contact with. She had married her college sweetheart and spent several wonderful years with the love of her life; and now, when she'd least expected it, she'd found true love a second time. At that very moment, she felt like the Grinch, when his heart grew ten sizes. She hadn't realized that it was possible to love someone so completely; yet have it feel so different than the love she'd shared with Jared. And finally it dawned on her that all the feelings that she had been experiencing with Aedan were simply part of being in love with the man. And that thought made her happy and finally content.

Danielle and Gwen showed up as she sat at the kitchen table, reading Aedan's note yet again. Hearing her dog bark, she jumped up and quickly got her work clothes on, and took one bite of her donut as they came inside. They looked as terrible as she felt. She said nothing but walked back into her kitchen and retrieved more donuts for her partners in crime. Gwen didn't say a word but devoured it in less than four bites.

"Where is your daughter Gwen?"

"Oh shit! I knew I was forgetting something." She said, looking serious. "Actually, Samantha volunteered to watch her for me today if I'd make her a pair of earrings and a bracelet to match," she confessed, finishing the last crumbs of her donut.

"Ladies, I believe that we have company," Danielle said as she heard before she saw the influx of vehicles making their way down Nicole's drive. Only Moriah and Star, along with Rainy and two others came via horseback. The other women from the village came the slower, but warmer and dryer route. Danielle went outside to meet her friends who were already unloading their buckets and tools to harvest what was left of their gardens. She was greeted warmly but in the reserved manner that the people of Destiny were always known for.

Rainy jumped off the horse that she was riding with her mother and immediately ran to Nicole's side, hugging her warmly. Before she could even greet the child, she heard a distinctive yelp and then Neiko's bark. She felt her heart warm as she saw Sinjin come running toward her as well, practically jumping into her arms that were still holding Rainy.

"She wanted to come too Miss Nicole. I hope that is okay," the child said.

"Of course it's okay Miss Rainbow. You and your pup are welcome here anytime."

"And you are welcome in Destiny anytime as well. My poppa told me that and my grandma said that you'll be coming home soon and we're to make you welcome." Not sure quite what the child or Moriah might have meant by that statement, Nicole quickly dismissed it and welcomed Star and her mother as they made their way to the cabin.

"Good morning Nicole, Danielle," Moriah spoke casually. I brought you and your friend some tea this morning. I know it's an early start for a Sunday morning and I think this might make you feel better."

Forgetting her manners momentarily, Nicole snapped out of it and remembered to introduce her best friend to Rainy's mother and grandmother. When Gwen stepped forward to greet Nicole and Danielle's friends from across the river, she looked up at Moriah and into the eyes of elder woman and froze. She knew those eyes, she thought to herself but couldn't place them; but was certain that she had seen them before. Moriah looked back at Gwen as if knowing what she was thinking and greeted her warmly.

"Welcome to our piece of heaven. If you are a dear friend of our Nicole's, then you, your man and your daughter are welcome in our community as well."

Always somewhat on guard, Nicole quickly spoke up.

"Moriah, how did you know that Gwen has a daughter? No one said anything about her having a child."

"She glows of motherhood Nicole. She is a woman whose life is complete, just as yours and Danielle's is becoming. Besides," she winked, "I overheard you asking Samantha if she'd watch the child. Oh, and by the way, she would have done it for just the pair of earrings. She got you when you agreed to make her a bracelet as well," she added. "But your child is in good hands with the girl so I guess it is worth a couple of trinkets isn't it?"

Still perplexed why the woman looked so familiar, Gwen nodded in agreement. Then the subject was dropped as Moriah asked if she could go inside to boil the water for the tea that she'd brought for her hungover friends. Nicole started to ask how she'd known they were a little out of sorts this morning but decided just to let it go as it seemed Moriah usually knew more about herself than she did sometimes.

All together there were eleven women working in the greenhouse and harvesting the last remnants of potatoes from the garden. Many hands made light work and as the morning progressed, they wrapped up the last bit of work that needed to be done. Once completed, some of the villagers from Destiny said their goodbyes and went on their way, but not before promising to return late afternoon for the cookout that Nicole still insisted on having. The women were told to bring something to pass and folding chairs to sit on and Nicole and Gwen promised to take care of the rest. Moriah, Star and only a few other women remained behind. Even for a fall day, the sun remained warm by northern New Hampshire standards and everyone enjoyed eating their lunch under the shade of one of the many trees that dotted her yard. The river could be heard in the distance and Gwen realized quickly how Nicole could feel at home and at peace in an environment such as this. They all made small talk with the topics of discussion jumping from subject to subject. Finally, Danielle decided to go all out and ask something that had been on her mind for several days now.

"Star, I was wondering if I could ask you something and please keep in mind that we're friends regardless of your answer."

Feeling suddenly on edge, she responded.

"Sure Danielle, what did you want to ask?" Moriah reached over and squeezed her daughter's hand.

"Um, well, you've been a friend of mine for some time now, and I don't have any siblings, other than Aedan and he's certainly not a girl, and well, you're Bruce's sister, whether you still acknowledge it or not. I love your brother with every ounce of my heart and soul. What I'm trying to say is, I was wondering if you'd consider standing up with me when I marry your brother? You'd be a bridesmaid I guess, in an unconventional sense of the word since there's nothing conventional about the wedding we're planning. Nicole has already said yes, and I'm hoping that you," she said, looking from Star to Gwen, "and Gwen would be my bridesmaids."

Both women screamed "Yes" simultaneously and dove towards Danielle, smothering her in a massive bear hug. Moriah sat by, and smiled, watching her family grow.

Chapter 39

After the last women left, Danielle offered to go into town to pick up some essentials for the party. She had already pulled out enough meat to feed an army and when Nicole objected stating that they couldn't take all of her beef, Danielle laughed and corrected her, informing her that it was venison and was just part of one of the deer that they'd tagged the previous season. Nicole quickly reminded herself that she wasn't in Kansas anymore and that when in Rome so to speak, do as the Roman's do. She smiled and told Danielle that she liked venison and would be happy to whip some of it into chili if she could get her hands on some kidney beans. Danielle obliged her with one very large can of beans, along with fresh lima beans as well. "Throw them in together and they'll complement each other Nic," she said optimistically.

"Okay, if you say so, but if my chili stinks, then I'm blaming you for making me add lima beans," she teased as she washed some of the many cayenne peppers they'd just harvested from the greenhouse. Gwen reminded them both that she was an absolutely horrid cook and would tackle making a massive salad, a feat she felt safe performing. Both chuckled and agreed as Danielle made her way toward the door and her truck.

"Call me if you think of anything else that you need," she shouted back to Nicole as she got into her truck.

"Will do. And thanks for agreeing to help me with this cookout Danielle. Something tells me that bringing both sides of the river together has been a long time in coming and needs to happen tonight."

"Don't start getting all voo doo mystic on me Nicole or you'll start sounding like Moriah. How about we just enjoy a great cookout with friends and then let everyone go back to their separate lives ok? The division between the two communities didn't occur overnight and it won't be fixed over a cookout either. So let's agree to disagree as to whose lifestyle is better; okay?"

"Absolutely," Nicole smiled back, with her fingers crossed behind her back.

Excitement was growing on both sides of the river. In Destiny, the men were finishing up the last of the trees and everyone felt confident that they'd cut enough to last them another year. Realizing that the wood they cut this year would be used the following year, Aedan wondered how full everyone's basements and garages were and if he and Nicole had stacked enough in their basement to last the winter. He reminded himself to speak to Bruce and Danielle about their supply when he returned home.

Home, he loved the sound of the word and with Nicole there waiting for him, it sounded even sweeter.

Bruce and Jimmy joined him to load up and return back to Mystique River. They were sweaty, exhausted and anxious to see their women; but all felt a sense of accomplishment. Small talk was minimal. Just before they reached Aedan's home, Jimmy spoke.

"Hey Bruce, Gwen and I were talking; and we were sort of wondering since you don't have a lot of family so to speak, if there would be any possibility that we might be able to invade your special weekend. We know you're getting married on a Friday night. Well, we were thinking that maybe if we came back up here in six weeks and got married on Saturday, and my entire family joined us for the ceremony, well maybe they all could be in attendance at yours as well. Even though they don't know you yet, they all feel as if they do since you helped deliver their niece and my parent's granddaughter. I know Gwen and I had planned on a spring wedding, but we've already got the rings, the money and the baby, and we were sort of talking last night and thought what the hell. If you think Danielle, or you for that matter, feel like we'd be encroaching on your day, just say so, and we'll stick with our original plan."

Jimmy looked at Aedan and Bruce, waiting for any kind of response, with Aedan being the first to speak.

"Oh my God, he's become just like Nicole Rose! He can talk for a full minute using only one breathe, just like his sister!"

"I don't like the idea at all. I will speak with Danielle but I know what she's going to say as well."

Feeling somewhat foolish and very embarrassed, Jimmy felt himself turning red. He had thought that it was a good idea, and that he and Gwen had offered it for all the right reasons but it obviously was overstepping their bounds.

Bruce spoke as the saw his friends face drop.

"Danielle is going to say no way are you getting married on Saturday if we already have the town hall booked for Friday. She's going to tell you to get married on Friday with us and we'll have a double wedding! We'll be the talk of the town and it'll be the biggest party this place has had in a long time," he said smiling.

"You and our Gwenny want to get hitched up in this neck of the woods, then I say let's do it all together; and yes, I'd love for your family to become part of ours."

Both Aedan and Jimmy felt their breathing finally return back to normal as they digested his words. "That's very generous of you Bruce," Jimmy responded, "but you know how women can be. If we don't make it their day and their day only, they could potentially freak and we'll pay for it the rest of our married lives," he chuckled.

"Tell you what," Bruce said with a twinkle in his eye, "you talk to yours and I'll talk to mine and we'll discuss it at the cookout this evening."

"Deal," Jimmy responded. As they dropped Aedan off at his cabin, Jimmy shouted "You know Aedan; we could make it a triple wedding. Make an honest woman out of my sister," he laughed. Seeing Aedan flipping him the bird was enough to make them both bust out in laughter.

Chapter 40

He showered, changed and dove in helping Nicole prepare the last of the food for the informal cookout. No one anticipated a lavish affair, just burgers and dogs on the grill and some pot luck entrees that people whipped together. He'd like to say that he didn't give it another thought; but honestly, he couldn't get Jimmy's suggestion out of his head. It was a ridiculous thought, he knew that. But then why did he keep thinking about it and whether or not it had possibilities. No, he thought, why should he possibly mess up a good thing, a stable thing, by asking her to marry him. He saw where the last engagement went; right down the toilet and he didn't want anything, to potentially jeopardize the relationship that he had with Nicole. Besides, he told himself, he'd only known her for months, not years. She had already said, on numerous occasions, that she'd never get married again, so it was a moot conversation that he was currently having with himself.

Nicole could tell that something was eating at him but didn't know what it was. He seemed very preoccupied and she could have sworn that she'd heard him talking to himself. Sure, he'd done anything she'd asked to help prepare the meal that she was making, but something was off and it bugged her to not know what it was. Bruce had been able to secure the town hall for their impromptu cookout and since they didn't really have any idea how many people would be in attendance, he thought it best to be prepared should a few dozen actually attend. Once Danielle was ready with her Venison patties, she swung by Nicole and Aedan's place to help Nicole load the chili and desserts that she'd somehow had time to make. Everything smelled appetizing as they loaded up the truck. Nicole, Jimmy and Gwen informed her that they'd be along shortly as they wanted to speak with Nicole alone for a moment or two before the festivities began. Once Danielle had headed down their drive, Gwen asked her best friend to sit down, which even though her serious expression was instantly putting her on alert, she did as asked.

"Nic, I need you to hear me, hear us out with what we'd like to talk to you about. None of it is spontaneous, well at least not 100% spur of the moment. It's all part of our long term plan, just tweaked a little bit so to speak."

Taking a deep breath, Gwen just blurted it out. "Jimmy and I are getting married!" Nicole had already known that they were planning on tying the knot in the spring so she wasn't quite sure what the excitement was about. "I know Gwen, you told me that you were getting married next spring. Don't you remember that conversation? We just talked about it the other day."

"I remember it very well Nicole," she responded. "That was then, this is now. Jimmy and I aren't waiting until next spring! We're getting married in a dual ceremony with Danielle and Bruce, here, in six weeks! Isn't that awesome? And both Danielle and I insist that you stand up for us. Unless of course you and Aedan want to get hitched at the same time and we can make it a threesome?" Nicole almost spit out her diet coke when she heard Gwen's suggestion.

"Thanks, but I'm good. Been there, done that. Never doing it again." Then she looked up and into the eyes of the man who'd captured her heart, and realized that he'd heard the entire conversation. He said nothing, turned and exited the room, but not before she saw his expression.

The four of them drove into town, along with Lauren Rachel, who slept much of the way. The truck ride seemed to drag on forever with Nicole trying to make small talk with Aedan. He was nothing but polite, answering her questions when short but precise answers. He was friendly and pleasant but nothing more. It was as if he'd shut down inside, and Nicole realized that her flippant remark had been the catalyst.

Once they walked into the town hall, Danielle took one look at her brother and knew instantly something was terribly wrong. And when she saw the same pained expression on Nicole's face, she knew that whatever was eating at him was doing the same to her, and somehow that brought her a feeling of comfort. Deciding the best approach was to simply ask or ignore; she opted to act like she hadn't noticed anything.

"Hey guys," she said cheerfully, about time you got here! Everyone is gonna start rolling in here pretty soon so can you ladies help me finish setting up? Aedan, love, take that pot of chili from Nicole and set it over by Bruce. Ladies, follow me," she said turning on her heels and walking into the kitchen before they had a chance to respond. Aedan did as she asked, taking the crock pot from Nicole and once he lifted it from her, realized just how heavy it was. Finally looking directly into her eyes, he said sincerely, "Nic, why didn't you ask me to carry this. I had no idea it was so heavy. I'm sorry honey," he said absentmindedly.

Taking the opportunity, she never wavered in her eye contact and responded, "It's okay Aedan. And I'm the one who's sorry. What you walked in on and overheard was not what you thought it was. You only heard part of my response to Gwen. What you didn't hear was what was in my heart; and that is that if I was ever going to get married again, it would be to someone like you." Realizing that she truly wasn't getting through to him, she touched his arm slightly. "I love you Aedan, so please don't shut me out. You misunderstood what you heard or thought you heard. So you can either accept what I'm saying or you can continue to sulk all day; choice is yours."

"No Nic, you know how I feel, the choice has always been yours." And with that he walked away from her for the second time in less than an hour.

Chapter 41

Nicole and Gwen thought that they might have a dozen or so people from both sides of the river actually show up for their impromptu cookout. When they saw Miranda and Deanna, and Jeremiah from the clinic, along with their families and significant others, they saw Ted and Mandy from the grocery store following close behind. As Nicole watched the slow but steady flow of people approaching the town hall, she quickly surmised that they were going to have a great turnout of towns' folk, but was slightly saddened when it appeared that the inhabitants of Destiny were going to pass on attending. Nicole greeted those she knew warmly, and introduced herself to those she didn't; and when there was a brief lull, she excused herself to go inside and check on the food preparation.

She heard what sounded like a stampede of horses coming from outside, and both she and Gwen looked at each other questioning the noise. Danielle smiled and simply announced that it sounded like the rest of their guests were arriving. Everyone made their way outside to see not only nine fully loaded trucks making their way into town, but also at least a dozen horses with both men and women on them. Nicole smiled recognizing Ellis' truck and its' inhabitants, with Rainy jumping out and running toward them as soon as it came to a stop.

"Hi, momma and Grandmamma got half the town to come over and enjoy the cookout with you Miss Nicole!" she said excitedly. "Everyone's talking about you and Doctor Aedan, saying you're a healer too, just like Grandmamma. The girls all think Doc Aedan is cute," she said blushing, "but I told them that he's hands off for two reasons," she continued. "One, he's not from Destiny, and two, he's in love with you," she smiled, and then ran off to join some of her friends.

Back in the kitchen, Danielle seized the moment. "He is you know," she added, after hearing the conversation between Nicole and the child. "My brother is not one to open up his heart and he's given it to you Nicole. I'm not sure what's going on with you two right now, but all I ask is that you don't hurt him."

"Gwen suggested that we get married the same time as you and Bruce, and she and Jimmy."

"I see," she said slowly. "And I take it that the concept of marrying my brother is repulsive to you?" she asked, choosing her words carefully but deliberately.

"Of course it's not repulsive Danielle," she replied, somewhat incensed that his sister would even imply such a thing.

"Then is it so far-fetched that your best friend, who's marrying your favorite brother, and are sharing their wedding day with Bruce and myself, with me being Aedan's only living relative; would want you to be part of what is going to be a very special day? I can understand if you don't really care about my brother. Shit, sex is sex, and a woman who looks like you can probably get it anywhere," she added, just to strike a few nerves.

"But my brother isn't like that; when he cares about someone, he gives his entire heart and soul and probably that's his downfall and why he's suffered when it comes to love. I know that he's 100% in love with you and whether he wanted to or not, he's fallen hard for you. So if you're just using him or it's some kind of game for you, I'm just asking that you let him down easy, ok?"

Now furious, she fired back.

"Maybe I would have considered it, if the man himself had mentioned it?" she almost screamed back at the woman standing in front of her. "And don't you dare, for one damn second think that what I feel for your brother has been some kind of game or that I'm using him. Hey, I never asked for him to enter my life. And I never asked or wanted him to permeate my heart, in fact, I fought it tooth and nail the entire time that he was being nice to me, saying the kindest things I've ever heard, showing me that it was okay to fall in love again for the second time in my life and actually start dreaming about a future with someone again. Your damn brother forced me to fall in love with him; and god damn it, I would marry him if he'd quit beating around the bush and actually ask me!" she said, slamming the ladle down on the counter and storming off. Aedan had been in the right place at the right time, and this time he heard the sincerity and truth behind her words. His heart burst with joy but his mind started spinning with what he was going to do with the information.

Not even a half hour into the spontaneous picnic, Nicole was pleasantly surprised to see that they'd nearly filled the town hall with families from both sides of the river. Everyone was mingling and making small talk, albeit tentatively at first; but both communities were sitting together and sharing one meal. The children from both sides of the river, most of whom had never met one another, played kick the can, tag and basketball, despite the crisp air outside. The men chatted about their recently completed tree and wood cutting party and the women talked about the men. They had enough food to feed the entire town, and by the looks of the hall, they'd be close to doing just that. Neither Aedan nor Nicole could hold a conversation without someone stopping by to thank them for their medical care, and for moving into their community. Nicole, who had always hated being the center of anyone's attention, felt uneasy every time she was approached but smiled and graciously accepted their well-meaning compliments. She glanced over at Aedan from time to time and saw that he was in good company with a nearly continuous flow of women making their way over to him. Danielle wasn't helping any, as she was by his side introducing him to all of them, like he was some prized steer available for slaughter. Chastising herself for her jealousy, she squared up her shoulders, excused herself from the women that were talking her ear off, and made her way toward him. As she approached, he looked up at her and she couldn't help but think that he had the look of a cat that'd just eaten the prized canary. And then he smiled at her, dimples and all.

"Aedan, I'm sorry to interrupt," she said in the sweetest syrupy voice that she could muster; but I'm afraid you're needed right away. Can you come with me please?" she said, turning and walking away, leaving him no choice but to follow and leave the flock of women behind.

"What's wrong?" he asked as he followed her outside, trying to figure out what the issue or problem was. She didn't say a word until she was standing beside his antique truck Maude. She turned and grabbed him by the shirt, pulling him into her. She acted on impulse and desire, and drew him into a kiss passionate enough to create spontaneous combustion. She melted into the sweetness of his mouth against hers and allowed what she felt for him to flow from her in the form of a kiss. Though hesitant at first, he immediately took what was offered and drank it in. After what seemed like an eternity, they finally separated lips and still mesmerized by her actions, he waited for her to speak.

"You misunderstood me earlier Aedan. Do you understand how I feel about you now?"

Trying to keep his physical response to her kiss under control, he simply nodded.

"Good." And one more thing she added before she sashayed away, "If I were to ever get married again, it would only be to you; so if ever the thought crosses your mind Doc, you know what the answer will be." And this time it was her turn to walk away, leaving him speechless.

Chapter 42

The picnic lasted well into the night, despite the fact that they had a long bumpy road ahead of them to return home. Star, Moriah and several of the women of Destiny insisted on staying to help pick up. Everyone seemed to have had a great time visiting and getting to know each other a little better and in doing so, realized that both of their communities were trying to accomplish the same thing, which was to raise their families in a community with structure, integrity and little governmental or outsider influence. Even the reluctant men like Ellis could be found laughing and actually relaxing a little, enjoying the food and beverages. Aedan, Bruce and Jimmy went from one group to another, with Bruce doing the introductions when necessary while Moriah watched on. She had longed for so many years to have her only son back in her life and seeing him now, so grown, so happy and so in love made her heart swell. Her son and daughter were all that she had left in this world, along with her granddaughter; and she silently rejoiced that she'd been given the opportunity to reconnect with him, and from outward appearances, appeared to have her communities support.

"Now if only she could somehow, someway find her long lost sister," she thought to herself as she watched her loved ones interacting. But that was a wish that she knew would go unfulfilled. And then it hit her.

Chapter 43

Morning came quickly for Nicole and Aedan, along with all the other townsfolk that had to work on a very cold Monday. The air felt like snow when Aedan rose early to put more wood in the stove. Refusing to admit that the cabin was freezing, he stoked the stove, and quickly jumped under the hot spray of the shower. Remembering that Nicole had asked if they could swing by his sisters to say good bye to her friend and brother, he showered and dressed, then called for her dog to let him outside to do his business. By the time he'd come back in, Nicole was already showered, dressed and making coffee. She never ceased to amaze him on how quickly she could get ready in the morning. All the other women in his life, his sister included, seemed to take forever to make themselves presentable for the day. Nicole always seemed to pull of an all-natural appearance and it was a look that Aedan liked, instead of a woman plastered in makeup. She handed him a cup of steaming coffee and smiled.

"Good morning. Thought you might need this on a morning like this. It must be close to freezing out there from the looks of my poor flowers."

"Yeah, not really a frost yet. But after the fantastic weather we've had so far this fall, it feels like it's subzero out," he joked. "Neiko's all set, so I'm ready when you are."

"Great! Just let me grab our lunches and I'll be ready. I hope Gwen is up because Lord knows she was slamming them down last night at the picnic."

"She has a baby now so my bet is that she's been up a lot longer than you think." They said their good-byes to her dog and took Maude, his truck over to his sisters where they met Jimmy loading up their overnight bags into his truck. Knowing there was no chance that he had a hangover, Nicole greeted her big brother with a smile. He told them to go inside and that Danielle, Bruce and Gwen were all in the kitchen fussing over his little princess. Nicole made her way toward the door, with Aedan lingering behind to speak with Jimmy in private. Once she was out of earshot, Aedan got right down to business with what he wanted to discuss with her brother. Not one to sugarcoat anything, he just asked what was on his mind.

"Hey, I wanted to talk to you before you head back to New York, and I know you're pressed for time, so I'll make this short and sweet."

Catching his attention by the tone in his usually calm voice, Jimmy looked up at the man standing beside him.

"I realize that your father is still very much alive, but he's not here and you are, so I'm just going to lay it out for you. I intend to marry your sister and if I can convince her, then we'll be standing alongside you and Gwen and my sister and Bruce. I don't know if I can get her to commit that fast but that's my plan and I need to hear from you right now if you have any issue or problem with me marrying your kid sister?"

When Jimmy didn't immediately respond, Aedan felt his pulse rate quicken slightly and continued on. "Of course I am planning on contacting your father to ask for her hand in marriage but since you were here and have gotten to know me best, I thought I'd run the idea past you first to see what you think."

Choosing his words carefully, Jimmy looked into the eyes of the man standing before him. "Is that so?" He led off with. "And I assume my sister has no idea that that's what you're thinking and planning? I might not be a doctor, nor the brightest bulb in the box, but I have heard that brides to be usually like to have a say in planning their own weddings."

"While that's usually true for most brides," Aedan countered, "Your sister is not like ordinary women, and besides, she's already had her fairytale wedding. I'm not Jared, nor do I want to attempt to replicate their wedding or attempt to take his place. What they had was special and not to be forgotten; but I think what we have was meant to be and we both have been through hell and back trying to get to where we are now. And whether that stubborn sister of yours marries me or not is a moot point because she's invaded my life, my heart and every thought that runs through my mind each and every day and I could never go back to living life the way it was before I met her. So whether she wants to exchange rings or not is up to her; I just want to make sure you and the rest of your family know my intentions."

Jimmy digested what he had just heard, and even though he already knew it for fact, he appreciated the ex-soldier putting his heart on his sleeve and inadvertently asking permission to marry his kid sister. He absolutely approved of their union but wasn't quite ready to let Aedan off the hook just yet.

"I see," he said casually. "You love her correct? And I assume you'd do anything to make her happy? I already know you'd do anything to keep her safe; as evidenced by what happened up in Maine this past summer. And with you being a doctor and veteran and all, I'm going to assume that you didn't hook up with my kid sister for any financial gain, so I won't even insult you by mentioning it. So, I guess I have only one question for you." Aedan waited to hear what the question could possibly be. "Nicole won't come right out and admit it, but the one thing that she has never accomplished and has eluded her due to no fault of her own, is having children. She has always wanted to have children and I need to know that if you marry my sister, you'll have to want them too."

That was one topic that Aedan had never really given any thought to, had never really considered because he'd never gotten to that point in any relationship to consider it. Kids of his own? Shit that thought added a whole new angle to what was a great relationship. But then a thousand pictures swirled through his head of what life would be like with Nicole and his children, their children. He envisioned camping trips, and fishing by the stream, an auburn or maybe strawberry blonde little girl with eyes the color of the sea like her momma riding on his shoulders as they climbed a mountain. He envisioned their sons playing with Neiko or any other strays that came their way that Nicole felt she needed to rescue, sitting on bleachers for their various sporting events, and the list went on and on. He felt a rush of heat flowing through him as if a dam had just been opened to the possibilities of what life could be for him and embraced it, welcomed it and instantly prayed for it.

Smiling, he looked at his future brother-in-law and simply replied. "Yeah I think two or three kids is doable."

Jimmy extended his hand. "Well then, welcome to the family. But do me a favor; let me give you Pa's number just so you can officially ask him. You know, Nicole's his only baby girl and he'll want to drill you even worse than I did," he winked.

"Our momma is going to well up something fierce when she hears the news," he added, still shaking Aedan's hand.

"Well then I might want to get around to asking Nicole pretty soon before she hears it from someone else," he chuckled as he saw Gwen, Danielle and Nicole exiting the cabin and heading their way. Gwen instantly knew they were up to something and by the smile on Aedan's face, she knew it involved her best friend.

Everyone hugged and kissed and said their good-byes with Gwen promising to ship up all of the bracelets and earrings that she had on hand back home in Syracuse. Knowing they'd see each other in less than six weeks made their departure less painful and once Lauren was secured in her car seat, they headed out so that Aedan and Nicole could get to the clinic on time. Once they'd left, Nicole and Aedan also said their goodbyes and headed toward town to start their work week. They rode in relative silence much of the way, with Aedan making small talk occasionally.

"Hey," he said casually, "I think it's kind of cool that Jimmy and Gwen are committing themselves to one another at the same time as my sister and Bruce. It'll be a special day for all to remember. I, for one, am happy for all of them. Maybe Gwen wasn't too far off base Nic. Maybe we should consider participating in their ceremony too." As soon as he heard the words come out, not necessarily as he had anticipated they would, he saw her body tense and knew he'd crossed a forbidden line.

Gently, she blew him off.

"That is such a sweet gesture Aedan, and I appreciate the offer but you're just getting caught up in the moment when we should just be happy for the four of them. Is what we have between us so unstable that we need to put rings on a certain finger on our left hands to prove that we're a couple?" Not giving him time to respond, she continued, "I think that you know me well enough by now to realize that I don't need to get married again just to prove that I love you." And with that, she exited the truck, leaving a bewildered Aedan sitting in the cab alone. "Well, Ms. Brentwood, we'll see about that," he thought to himself. "I plan on marrying you and having babies with you. You might want to get used to that fact sooner rather than later," he said to himself as he exited his truck and started to follow her in.

He hadn't taken two steps toward the clinic when Moriah turned the corner and nearly walked into him. Startled he looked down into the petite woman's eyes and tried to read what those weary eyes held. Immediately feeling the energy that she was giving off, she quickly reassured him that nothing was wrong and that actually, everything was right and coming together the way it was meant to. She explained that she was on her way to the store to pick up a few essentials that they'd forgotten when they were in town yesterday. Before saying goodbye, she reached into the weathered pocket of her khaki skirt and pulled something out. "I've been meaning to give this to you," she said, extending out her hand towards him.

Not knowing what she had, he put out his hand willingly to receive her gift. She handed him the stone that she'd kept in her possession until the time was right. She knew that the time had come and that he would be receptive to it. He felt its energy before he looked down at what she'd placed in his hand. It looked and felt like an ordinary rock, except for its unusual pink color. "What is it?" he asked, genuinely confused.

"It's called a Pink Sapphire, kunzite, rose quartz or Morganite. It's the stone symbolizing eternal, never-ending love for souls destined to be together. It was given to me by my sister years ago for safe keeping and now I'm giving it to you. Do with it what you will. Maybe it'd make a great paperweight, or an addition to your fish tank," she said as she turned to leave.

"I just know that it was meant to be given to you at this time. Any maybe, just maybe," she said as she started walking away, "It could be cut down and shaped into a beautiful stone for a special woman. Maybe that's what it was meant to be all along," she shouted back as she rounded the corner and out of sight.

Aedan looked down at what he held in his hand and knew exactly what he was going to do with it, as he slipped it into his pocket and went inside to start the morning.

Chapter 44

The next few weeks flew by without incident with most of their patients having pretty straightforward ailments or injuries. Nicole had started running with her dog every morning since the evenings were getting shorter and colder. Once she left every morning for her run, Aedan was on the phone. Twice in the last two weeks, she'd come back to find him talking away, and as soon as she entered their cabin, he abruptly ended his conversation with whomever was on the other end. Not one to be jealous but nature, she was more curious than jealous about who he could be talking with at such an early hour but didn't want to pry. She spoke with her family frequently and he never interrupted or asked about their topics of conversation so she wasn't going to start on him about his.

Miranda, Deanna and Jeremiah were finally used to the way that she and Aedan worked together and Nicole had noticed how much more relaxed they seemed to be around her. Miranda was still on her soapbox about the end of the world as they knew it but Aedan listened to her rants with interest and to a degree thought that her fatalist mentality had some merit though he didn't honestly feel that any country had the ability to bring their threats to fruition. He did, in fact believe that there would be more lone wolf attacks throughout the nation

313

but couldn't honestly put much credence in what Miranda felt was going to occur in the near future. He gave Nicole credit for listening during their lunch breaks to Miranda and occasionally Jeremiah's views about how they thought extremists, whether foreign or homegrown, would attack the country someday and what, in their opinion, everyone should be doing to prepare. Deanna could be seen rolling her eyes on more than one occasion as Miranda went off on her tangents but never argued with her co-workers because deep down, she agreed with majority of her concerns.

Aedan and Nicole spent their evenings reading and enjoying the solitude of their cabin in the woods. They worked together, shared the chores both inside and outside equally, with Nicole using an ax to split wood almost as proficiently as Aedan, and spent their evenings together as well. Rarely did they disagree on topics of discussion, except when discussing where their relationship was going. Nicole used a standard answer that although she loved him, she couldn't think about committing to someone so soon; which Aedan knew was an answer of convenience and not necessarily a truthful one. He'd spoken with both her father and mother, asking their permission to marry their daughter, to which they both happily agreed. He had spoken with each and every one of her siblings once they'd gotten wind of his intentions, with each offering their opinions, comments and instructions on how to make her come around to his way of thinking. He was very happy to have all of them on his side. Now he just had to convince her and he was down to two weeks to get it done. At least he'd been able to get his sister involved in some of the planning. When Danielle had insisted that Nicole come with her dress shopping, she had reluctantly agreed. Seizing the moment, Danielle had pretty much strong-armed her friend into purchasing a gorgeous full length dress to wear on Danielle's wedding day, with Nicole having no idea that Danielle was in fact helping her pick out a dress that she too would be getting married in; that is, if Aedan could convince her to marry him. Seeing her in the light sea foam green dress with frilly chiffon layering reminded Danielle of a fairy with Nicole's long billowy hair flowing over her shoulders. When she turned in a 360, she looked like a goddess, and Danielle knew that her twin would be mesmerized that day and for the rest of his life. When Nicole questioned Danielle on her choice of attire for her wedding day, her response was that she'd never been a conformist and wasn't going to start on her wedding day. She'd chosen a turquoise blue dress for her wedding dress because it matched the color of her eyes and to be rest assured that her bra and panties would be white so she'd have something virginal in color on, a comment that caused Nicole to burst out laughing. Gwen, being her usual flamboyant self, had chosen a very bright coral color for her dress. It was strapless and showcased her figure very well, which was toned and physically fit, despite having had a baby not that long ago. Neither bride chose to wear a traditional white wedding dress but somehow it just seemed natural that both would showcase their individual personalities in the dresses that they'd chosen for their big day. The town hall would be where both their ceremony and reception would be held. Both Gwen and Danielle had insisted on just having a casual family style reception after their commitment ceremony. Neither was looking for a traditional wedding or reception, and while Nicole respected their decision, she hoped that neither would someday regret not having their big day be more formal, like hers had been when she wed Jared so long ago. Thinking back now, it seemed like light years ago and so much had changed in her life since she was a young blushing bride. She'd had her formal wedding and couldn't help but think that if she were to do it again, she'd probably do it exactly like her two best friends were about to do.

The weekend rolled around and Nicole had mentioned to Aedan earlier in the week that she'd like to take Neiko for a hike before the snow finally started falling. He hadn't committed nor said no, so she'd dropped the subject. When she found herself awake and alone on a gorgeous sunny Saturday morning, she decided to take advantage of the weather and go for a quick hike on her own. She packed a lunch, water for herself and her dog, her 9mm and the other essentials that she always kept in her backpack and took off in her truck towards the mountains. As she was heading on down the road, she realized that she'd forgotten to leave him a note, but when she checked her phone and saw that she had cell coverage in the area where she was heading, she didn't worry about it, and thought she'd just text him once she got to her destination.

They'd gotten an early start that morning as he and Bruce drove into Errol. The jewelry store opened at 9am and they wanted to be there and back before their women became suspicious. Aedan was anxious to see what the jeweler had done with the stone. He went on a leap of faith when the owner of the shop had promised him that not only could he make the quartz into a stunning ring, but that it would be one of a kind; and that was what Aedan was banking on. But now, driving into Errol, his stomach was in knots as he began to reconsider his impulsive decision.

"What if she hates it, what if she says no, what if it doesn't turn out like I envision it will?" he thought to himself. Noticing his white knuckles tightly clenched on the steering wheel, Bruce reached up and touched his shoulder. "Relax. She's going to love it. She might kick your ass for the way you're about to ambush her into marrying you, but she's going love the ring."

"Thanks for the vote of confidence buddy."

"No problem. My pleasure," he responded back, opening the door to the jewelry store.

Once inside, both men paced anxiously. Bruce for the wedding bands that Danielle had sent him to pick up and also for the specially made necklace that he'd had designed; while Aedan just wanted to see if the raw piece of Rose Quartz could actually be turned into a ring worthy of such a unique woman. He knew that he could pick out a diamond solitaire today if the pink stone didn't meet his expectations but he truly wanted to give her something one of a kind and at the time that he'd dropped the stone off, he'd thought it a good idea. Now, he was virtually sick to his stomach with nerves as he waited to see the finished product.

When the sales clerk returned from the back room with Bruce's purchase, Aedan peeked over his shoulder to check out the wedding band that would be on his sister's finger in a matter of days, and smiled approvingly. He felt his heart quicken as the store manager approached him with a small plain white box. Saying nothing, he gave it to Aedan who was almost afraid to lift the lid, afraid that it might not be what he was looking for. And it wasn't. It was the most intricate and unusual ring that he'd ever seen in his life and the way that the white gold was delicately wrapped around the cut of the stone reminded him of vines on a tree enveloping something precious that they wanted to hold and care for forever. The quartz had been cut into an emerald cut with the four edges being secured in place by the white gold. The ring was not large in size, as he'd worried that it might be, but would complement the size of her finger perfectly. As he held the ring up to look at the detailing on the sides of the ring, he saw how it caught the sunlight and seemed to draw it into the stone. "Yes, he thought, this would do. This is the perfect ring for such a perfect woman."

"Hey Aedan," Bruce called, interrupting Aedan's train of thought.

"That is one cool ring. Not sure what that's gonna set you back, but I'm guessing that she'll say yes when she sees it. You did a great job designing it and Nicole's going to love it."

"I have to agree with the gentleman sir," the store manager said. "I've never seen anything quite like it and your lady is sure to love it. May I ask, how did you come to acquire the quartz? It is a near perfect rock with no noticeable imperfections, even under the microscope. Quartz like that is not indigenous to our area, yet it looks like it had been protected by the earth until you brought it in to us to be made into your ring. It's an absolutely stunning specimen."

Feeling awkward now that he'd probably diminished the value of the Quartz that Moriah had given him by having it cut down to make the ring for Nicole, he simply replied that it had been given to him. Bruce eyed him suspiciously but said nothing. The four continued to make small talk with the TV playing in the background. Suddenly the young sales clerk gasped, drawing all of their attention to the TV screen. The TV had stopped its regular broadcast, stating that there had been multiple train derailments in the metro Atlanta area and that part of the subway system was also down, with no cause stated. The story was just unfolding with little details known at the time. The four men kept their eyes glued to the screen. The news reporter was panicky and her report was without much information except that the trains had jumped their tracks and derailed, with no word on casualties yet. She then went on to say that three of the 36 subway stations in operation in the greater Atlanta area had instantaneously lost their computer systems and that representatives from MARTA rail system could not be reached for comment with no cause being identified at that time. She went on to report that the area hadn't suffered any earthquakes and that the cause was unknown at this time. Once the TV eventually went back to its regular programming, the men and women who had congregated in the tiny jewelry store to listen to the shocking news, all looked at one another in silent disbelief. Bruce and Aedan promptly paid their bills and excused themselves, wanting nothing more than to get home to their women.

Both Aedan and Bruce tried to contact their respective loves, with neither being successful. Both left voice messages but neither felt comfortable not being able to reach them. Aedan subconsciously accelerated and continued to attempt to reach Nicole, to no avail.

Chapter 45

Nicole and Neiko made excellent time up the mountain that she'd chosen for her climb. It had only taken them less than two hours of steading climbing to reach the summit. As both she and her dog relaxed eating their lunches in the warmth of a beautiful fall day, she pulled out her back pack to take a few pictures and touch base with Aedan. She took only a few pictures of the panoramic views around her and decided to head back down once she realized that she didn't have any reception on that side of the mountain. She had the feeling that something was wrong, but she couldn't quite pinpoint what it was. She finished up her lunch, knowing that she'd feel better once she could hear his voice.

What had taken her not quite two hours to scale, took her less than 60 minutes to descend with she and Neiko practically jogging in several spots. She was covered in sweat despite an air temperature barely in the 50's, and both she and her dog drank heartedly once back inside their truck. Finally in an area where she had reception, her phone lit up with all of the missed calls and texts that she had; majority of them from Aedan. She immediately thought of her parents and with shaking fingers, dialed his number, with him answering before the second ring.

"Where the fuck are you?" he practically screamed into the phone, so relieved to hear her voice but so frustrated that it had taken until now for her to call him back.

"Excuse me?" she said in a voice dripping with sarcasm. "I'm just leaving Elephant Mountain, you know, the one I invited you to climb with me this morning but you didn't bother to answer me either way."

Immediately remembering her mentioning the fact that she had wanted to hike today, their conversation came rushing back to him, leaving him feeling like a fool for worrying and like a heel for not going with her. Trying to calm his voice down before he spoke again, he took a deep breath and responded.

"Oh that's right. I'm sorry, I totally forgot that you'd planned on going this Saturday. So how was it," he asked cheerfully.

Nicole saw right through his act, even though she wasn't face to face with him, but she played along anyways.

"It was very nice and Neiko and I had a very good workout. So what have you been doing all day," she asked with the same bullshit sincerity that he'd just given her.

Stammering momentarily, he replied, "Oh Bruce and I are just on our way back from Errol. He had to pick up their rings and he wanted company, so I tagged along."

Unable to restrain herself, she flippantly responded back.

"Yeah, I kind of wanted company today too."

Hearing the disappointment in her voice, but also the sarcasm, he truly didn't know what to say to make the situation better so for the moment, he simply said "Sorry."

"Why were you texting and calling me so many times anyways," she asked, not quite ready to forgive him for blowing her off.

"Oh, Jesus. You don't know do you," he said realizing that she must have been in a no coverage zone the entire time and obviously hadn't turned her radio on in her truck yet. "There's been a multi train car derailment in Atlanta this morning and also, part of their subway computer system crashed, stranding hundreds underground in midtown Atlanta. How long before you're back to Mystique River?" he asked cautiously.

"About 40 minutes tops why?" she asked. "That's horrible about the train and the subway! Do they have any idea how it happened or what's going on," she asked, now solely focused on their topic of discussion and not so much on the fact that Aedan had blown her off.

"No. They're investigating but they don't have a cause at this time, nor has anyone claimed responsibility if it was done deliberately. Just come home okay," he said, with raw emotion evident in his voice.

"I'm on my way Aedan," and then the line went dead.

Chapter 46

He dropped Bruce off, barely acknowledging his sister when she invited him in, threw his truck in reverse and headed toward the tiny cabin that he and Nicole had made their temporary home. Usually careful not to kick up stones when he drove his pride and joy, at the moment he didn't care, didn't honestly care as he barreled down the long drive to what awaited him there. The second he saw her open the door for him with a welcome smile, he finally sighed a breath of relief. There, in front of him what everything he'd ever wanted, ever needed, and knew he could never live without. At her side was her beloved dog, and even though he was not necessary a dog person, he too had grown to love her four legged best friend. Her smile and stance told him that she was also glad that he was home and neither said a word, just started walking toward each other. He took the longest strides that his prosthetic leg would allow him to take and when they met in the yard, he took her into his arms and held on tight.

"Ah Nicki, the second I heard the TV telling about the disaster down in Atlanta, all I could think of was you, and getting back to you. And then you didn't answer you phone or return my texts, it left a pit in my stomach and it started messing with my head and everything that Miranda at work has been preaching about came rushing back and I didn't know where you were and it horrified me, simply undid me," he confessed.

Separating herself enough to look at the man who was holding onto her for dear life, she smiled as she lifted his chin.

"Look at me Aedan.   Look into my eyes and know what I say is true.   No one and nothing would keep me from getting back to you.   I'm right here and I'm not going any place and I'm not planning on leaving you so you'd better get used to that concept okay?"

Listening to what she was saying, he seized the moment and before he knew what he was doing, it just happened. He separated himself from her embrace and laughed a slightly devious sounding laugh.

"Hold that thought.   I'll be right back."   And before she could even respond or say a word, he was walking back to his truck and within a moment was returning with a tiny, fancy looking bag.   He was holding it like it was a rare, delicate piece of glass that would shatter with the slightest jarring and suddenly the easy going man that she'd grown accustomed too looked all nerves and all business.   He walked back to her and without saying a word, leaned in and kissed her, simply kissed her with every emotion possible flowing between them as their lips met.   They kissed for what seemed like eternity and then they separated, he reached for her hand. "Nicole Rose Brentwood, when I heard that the world was going crazy and I couldn't reach you, I felt like I was dying inside. I don't have everything you're probably looking for in a man, nor do I pretend to know how to be a good husband but," he continued as he saw the color draining from her face. "The one thing I do know is how to love you, and I love you with every ounce of my being. I might not have been married before and I don't know if I'll be a good husband and father or not, but I would really like the opportunity to see if I am marrying material or not."

He carefully lifted the box out of the bag and handed it to her, saying nothing. She looked at the box he was holding to her and felt her hand shaking as she reached for it, knowing full well what must be in it. She looked into his eyes and in a voice barely above a quiver said, "You really don't want to be doing this, you really don't," looking up at him with eyes that bordered between terrified and nervous.

Seeing her expression, he actually felt satisfied that she was nervous and terrified at the same time.

"Please say yes Nicole. Please say you'll marry me Nicole Rose Brentwood. You don't have to commit to when and where, just say yes. Say yes that someday you'll take my name and be my wife."

Not sure if she too was caught up in the moment or not, she too reacted on impulse. She took one quick breath and simply nodded. He watched the movement of her head and couldn't believe what he was seeing. She was slowly but steadily nodding yes. He saw the smile come across her face and then he heard her voice say just one word, the one that he'd never forget for the rest of his life. "Yes. Yes Aedan, I will marry you."

Tears ran down her face as she heard herself say what she never expected to say to anyone ever again.

"Yes, someday I will become your wife but for right now, know that I'll always be by your side, and that's all that matters right?"

"Right," he said carefully. But I was sort of, maybe, possibly," he said, with both dimples showing, hoping that you might consider marrying me when Danny marries Bruce and your brother marries Gwen. And if that is even a possibility, I was hoping that you'd accept this," he said opening the box that she still held in her hand. She gazed down at the ring she was holding and started to shake. It was possibly the most beautiful thing she'd ever seen in her life. Even though she was absolutely terrified to accept what he was offering her, she lifted the ring out of the box and let the light bounce off it as it glistened in her hand.

"Try it on Nic. It's your size. My sister found out what size you wear and it should fit perfectly. Please try it on and let me know if you like it. I wanted something special and as unique as you are. But if you want a diamond, we can pick one out." Realizing that he was rambling, he looked into her eyes and tried to read her mind. She didn't know what to say, and just when she was about to answer him, she looked up and saw a lone hawk circling overhead. Knowing it somehow was a sign from Jared, she watched it soar and glide. She looked back at him and then again up at the hawk still overhead.

"I can't believe I'm saying this but yes, yes Aedan, I think I'd like to marry you when Jimmy marries Gwen and your sister marries Bruce! But how can we make that happen if it's only two weeks away? We don't even have a marriage license."

Now truly smiling, he laughed.

"Yeah, well about that, I might have sort of had Danielle forge your signature hoping that I could get you to say yes, so actually we do have a wedding license. Don't be mad okay?"

She couldn't believe what she was hearing but ironically, wasn't mad, shocked or surprised by his answer.

"Oh you did, did you? Anything else you already took care of?" she asked, still not putting the ring on a special finger on her left hand.

"Well, 'I've already asked your parents, who put me in touch with all of your brothers, who all gave me their blessings; along with a few very nasty threats should I ever hurt you or mistreat you," he added hesitantly, "and well Danielle might have, sort of been in on coercing you into buying a pretty dress that could double as a wedding dress. But other than that, no; that's it," he added, as he took the ring from her hand and slowly slid it onto her finger as she looked on but didn't stop him.

"Well," she said after she lifted her hand looking at the way it sparkled in the sunlight, "I guess you've thought of everything."

She reached out her hand and he took it immediately. "I'm not sure what kind of wife I'll be to you Aedan, I'm finally used to being a widow and not sure how good of a partner I'll make, but if you're willing to go for it, so am I."

"Sounds good to me. Any chance we can go inside now and celebrate?" he asked.

"We can go inside, but before we do any celebrating, let's take a few minutes so I can call my parents?"

"Sure. Are you afraid I didn't actually speak to your dad?"

"No silly! I just know that if I'm going to do this wedding thing again, I need to invite my parents and family and hope that they can make it on such short notice."

"Yeah, about that, they sort of already know the date, and are planning on attending. All of your brothers, along with your parents will be attending. They were going to make the trip for Jimmy's wedding and were thrilled when they heard it would hopefully turn into a double wedding for two of their children. Your mother's exact words were "son, if you can get Nicole to the alter, wild horses nor World War III couldn't keep us away."

"Yes, that sounds exactly like my mother alright. And you say all of my brothers and their families are coming? That's quite a gang you know. What about you Aedan, do you and Danielle have any family to invite? Or do you have any of your friends from the military that you'd like to invite?"

"Nope. We have a few distant cousins in Oregon and upstate New York, but no one who's going to make a trek half way across the country for our nuptials. After our parents died, it's pretty much always been just Danny and I. But hey," he said, taking her into his arms and kissing her gently.

"I have everything I could ever want or need right here in my arms. You complete me Nicki; absolutely complete everything that used to be missing."

Thinking about it, he had summed up everything that she felt; they completed each other and everything seemed whole when they were together.

"Let's go inside now honey."

And the celebrating began.

Chapter 47

As soon as they entered the clinic to start the work week, they could feel the tension in the air. Miranda was the first to greet them and without even asking if they'd heard, because she assumed they hadn't watched the news the night before; updated them on the situation in Atlanta. She went on to say that a group of extremists from Alzatar were claiming responsibility for both the explosion that caused the derailment of the trains and also for sabotaging the master control for the subway system on the line affected. Supposedly they were demanding the release of several of their military personnel that were being detained in the US and in Canada on war crimes and that they would continue to pick off targets all across both countries if their men and women weren't released. She went on to stress that the group claiming responsibility stated that the derailment and shutting down of the subway was only the beginning and tame compared to what would happen if their demands weren't met. Both Aedan and Nicole listened quietly, absorbing what their office manager was telling them. Nicole, usually the eternal optimist felt sorry for the people and their families affected by the train derailment and the men and women who perished in the accident, but didn't think much more about the incident except that it was senseless killing of innocent people. Aedan on the other hand took what Miranda was saying seriously, reminding himself to make contact with a few of his friends still in the military so that he could get a better understanding of what concerns there really were. Alzatar was a small country with what he thought was limited knowledge of biochemical and nuclear capabilities, but he would feel much more comfortable after he spoke with his contacts. Miranda went on to say that the extremists had given a deadline that was less than two weeks away. Nicole's ears perked up when she realized that the date was the day after their wedding. Then both Miranda and Deanna saw a new ring on a special finger on Nicole's hand, and almost simultaneously both shrieked in delight.

"Oh my God, you two finally did it! It's about time that you put a ring on her finger, and that is one hell of rock," Deanna exclaimed. "I've never seen a ring that color before Nic. What kind of stone is it? It's absolutely stunning!"

"It's a rose quartz Dee. I'm not sure where Aedan got it, but he had it designed by a jeweler in Errol. He's responsible for how incredibly unique it is, and I absolutely love it."

"It's gorgeous Nicole; it really is, congrats."

"Hey," Nicole said smiling, "I know this isn't formal or anything, but since the wedding is in less than two weeks,

I don't have time for formality. I just wanted to say that I'd really love it if you both, along with your significant others of course, could attend our wedding. I'm not asking because I'm expecting gifts; I'm asking because you are the only true friends that I have up here, and it wouldn't be the same if you weren't in attendance."

Kidding but semi-serious, Miranda said "Yeah Dee, we've become the substitute friends to replace all of the co-worker nurse friends she has back in New York that won't make the drive up here to the middle of nowhere," she laughed. Dee did not laugh as she saw the color drain out from Nicole's face. The room turned silent as she excused herself and practically ran out.

"What, I was just kidding," Miranda said, attempting to add levity to the atmosphere.

"Most of her co-worker nurse friends as you called them," Aedan said, in a lethal tone, "Were murdered when two gun men invaded her nursing unit and shot them to death." Turning to leave the break room and find Nicole, he added, "So yes, you have become her substitute friends and she values your friendships as much as she did theirs."

Once the room was empty except for Dee and Miranda, Deanna turned toward her co-worker and simply said, "Nice work you idiot."

Nicole blew everyone off as they tried to make light talk and get on with the day. The clinic was packed, which had become pretty much the norm since both she and Aedan were now officially considered part of the community. What amazed Nicole the most about the patients they saw was that everyone was always so appreciative for any care and/or advice they were given. Back in the hospital setting, far too often, the patients sometimes treated her and the other staff like servants, demanding this or demanding that, and many could be condescending or flat out rude at times. Not here, she realized. Every person who came to their clinic, whether they were young or old, male or female, treated all of the staff wonderfully and respectfully and genuinely was appreciative. She noticed that as the weeks had passed, even though it was still very few and very sporadic, they were beginning to see residents from both sides of the river. The townsfolk in Mystique River had for the most part, already accepted them, but it finally seemed that the residents of Destiny were accepting of them as well and that fact made Nicole smile to no end.

Just as the last patients were brought into the few remaining open examining rooms, Nicole looked up to see Ellis and young Joshua entering the reception area. Just when Deanna was about to tell them that they were closed for the day, Nicole stopped her. Smiling, she walked up to both man and boy.

"Hi guys. What a nice surprise to see you here. But I bet you must be feeling really awful to have made it all the way over to this side of town huh?" she said, looking directly into the child's eyes. He looked directly back at her and didn't say a word but nodded.

"Nicole, we think he really needs to see the doc. He's got white spots all across the back of his throat and where it's not white, it looks like his throat is on fire. It's red as hell. And he won't eat because it's too sore to swallow."

Nicole put her hand up to the child's forehead, and feeling the heat on his brow, already deduced that the child probably had strep throat, but she remained silent regarding her theory.

"Come with me okay and we'll find you a spot to hang out until Doctor Aedan can take a look at that nasty throat of yours. I'm just going to stick a quick Popsicle stick looking thing in to see what's growing back there okay?" Seeing the hesitancy in the child's eyes, she softly put her hands on his shoulders. "Joshua, would it be ok if my dog Neiko hung out with you until Doc comes in? I know he's really bored by this time of the day and I'm sure he'd love company. Do you think that would be okay?" Seeing the child's eyes light up told her the answer. He nodded yes, almost excitedly, forgetting about his sore throat momentarily. Knowing that her dog was sleeping in the kitchen and within earshot, Nicole whistled softly and within seconds, had the huge shepherd at her side. Seeing the dog immediately sit beside her, and lift his paw, as if in welcome, relaxed the child almost immediately. Then child, dog and uncle followed Nicole in to the exam room and waited to be seen.

When Joshua's rapid strep test came back positive almost instantaneously, Nicole realized just how raw his throat must feel, and went into their staff's kitchen, returning with a Popsicle for the child to enjoy while waiting. Aedan examined him shortly afterward and after making small talk about hunting, and other topics the child seemed interested in, handed them some antibiotic samples that he had in stock to treat the infection. Nicole instructed him to drink tea with honey at least twice a day and to gargle with licorice root mixed in water. The child heard the word licorice and thought of candy but then frowned when he heard that he was only going to mix the powder in water and rinse with it. Both Ellis and Aedan chuckled seeing the expression on his face. Wanting to change the subject, Nicole, in a serious tone asked Joshua if she could ask him a serious question, to which he nodded yes. Not quite sure what inspired her, she seized the moment.

"Joshua, I'm not sure if you know it or not, but Doctor Aedan and I are getting married this Friday night. Your Uncle Ellis and Aunt Star will be coming, along with Rainy and a few of the other people from your community. I don't have many friends, and I consider you and Gideon my friends, right?" she asked, pausing for the child to respond. He nodded yes so Nicole continued on. "So I was wondering if you both would like to accompany your aunt and uncle and join us for the party." Praying to hear his voice, but not surprised when he didn't speak, she smiled as he nodded yes and smiled.

"Good then, it's settled. We'll see you this coming Friday night. We're going to have a fun time. Oh, and Joshua, don't let your Aunt Star convince you that you, Gideon and Rainy have to wear some fancy smanchy clothes just because it's a wedding. You don't, just wear something comfortable that you can have fun in." Aedan smiled as he again nodded as he exited the exam room with Ellis in tow.

"That was a very nice gesture, inviting them to our wedding."

"I don't really think of it as our wedding honey. I honestly look at it as three weddings and a community celebration. It's not just about you and I. Yes it's about our new life together, but it's more about us marrying into this community, and the people in both communities coming together to celebrate new beginnings. That's the way I think of it. Tomorrow's never a given so we need to celebrate each and every day as if it's our last and as if it's the first day of a new life right?"

"Right. Now let's go home love because I'm hungry and tired."

"Let's go."

"Great, but on our way home, we need to make one really quick stop okay?"

"Sure, but you just said that you were hungry."

"I am but I wanted to show you something on our way home if you have the time. It'll only take a minute and if you don't like it, it'll take less than that," he said, as he helped her slip her coat on.

"Okay, deal. But what is it you want to show me?"

Smiling enough to show his dimples, he smiled.

"If I told you now, it wouldn't be a surprise now would it?"

"You're killing me Aedan."

"Come on, let's go. You're gonna love it!" he said as he opened the door, allowing Neiko to run outside and into the frigid air.

Aedan drove somewhat lost in his own thoughts but not second guessing what he was about to offer the love of his life. Nicole paid attention to the roads that they traveled on, some were marked with street signs, and others were not as they made their way out of town and away from their cabin. Just as they started their ascent up Elephant Mountain, Aedan made a sharp left hand turn down a bumpy dirt road and then a quick right into a driveway. Seconds later, he put his truck in park and told her to wait until he came around to open the door for her. She did as instructed, looking out at the stone and wooden home in front of her, wondering who lived there. The home was set on the side of the mountain and the way it was constructed made it look like the mountain grew around the home, not the other way around. Even with the waning sunlight, the view was spectacular as they made their way towards the front door. Thinking that someone would be opening the door to greet them at any moment, Nicole was somewhat surprised when Aedan reached into his jeans pocket and pulled out one lone key. She was even more astounded when he put it into the lock and opened the door, inviting her in.

"What is this place? Who lives here Aedan?" she asked, as she felt the hair starting to rise on the back of her arms.

"No one lives here anymore Nic. The owner passed away and the daughter no longer lives in the area. When I was in Errol, I inquired about homes that might possibly be for rent and this was one of them that I previewed. Since it was a great home and very reasonable to rent, I thought that it would be a lot more comfortable for your family to stay in than a hotel. I hope you don't mind, but I rented it for your parents and siblings for when they come up for our wedding, and Jimmy's of course," he added, trying to read her expression.

"You went ahead and rented a place for my entire family and didn't mention it to me first?" she said, still somewhat shocked. Not quite sure how to respond, he simply told her the truth.

"Yes. But why don't you at least take a look at the place and tell me what you think of it?"

"Okay, but why? It doesn't really matter what I think about it since it's someone else's home."

"True, but I would love to hear what you would do to it to change its appearance. I love the location but man is it outdated," he added casually.

Viewing the interior, she saw right away that the home had a very rustic country feel but also incorporated a modern feel with the rear wall of the main living space being floor to ceiling glass, accentuated with wrought iron. Her eyes followed the clean lines up to the ceiling that was done in a very dark hue tongue and groove. The dark against all that light made for a wonderful contrasting blend and then she saw the view outside. How could a home be anything but beautiful when its view was looking directly at a vast mountain range? Nicole also appreciated the wide barn planking that appeared to cover much of the first floor, including into the kitchen. Not one for tile, Nicole appreciated the fact that the owners had carried the wood all the way throughout and into the kitchen where against the white cabinetry, it made a bold statement. The double oven caught her eye, and the fact that all the appliances matched and were stainless steel didn't hurt either. She touched the countertops, trying to figure out what type of wood it was as she ran her hand gently over its surface. Aedan remained silent and just watched her as he knew the redecorating wheels in her head were already spinning. He walked toward the master bedroom with Nicole slowly following him as she absorbed everything around her as she walked behind him. He stepped aside as they got to the entrance and allowed her to enter first. When she did, she simply gasped at what she saw. The room looked like it had been designed and decorated in another era and preserved just that way. The massive wrought iron bed was set up directly in the middle of the room, with the amazing barn planking in it as well, but painted an antique white. The cherry end tables were miss matched but looked great together, and the massive chrome looking ceiling fan shouldn't work in a room with all of the ancient pieces, yet somehow it did. Again, the rear wall was a sea of glass looking out at the mountain range, with the fireplace that was on the opposite wall appearing to be made of local stone that could have been picked up on the very mountain side that she was now appreciating.

"Wow, you let my mother stay in this room, and I doubt you'll ever get her to leave," she said. "This home is quite spectacular. Who did you say owns this place?"

"I didn't say, why?" he said, now very curious as to what she was thinking.

"I'm just asking who owns it because whoever it is has extraordinary taste and style. There isn't a single thing that I'd change from what I've seen so far."

Seizing the moment, he smiled and motioned for her to check out the master bath, which he knew, would be her Achilles heel. Usually loquacious, she was speechless once she entered. Her eyes darted from the double sink fashioned out of an old dresser, to the massive stained glass octagon window, the fireplace taking up half of the wall, and finally to the old claw tooth bathtub which was the focal point of the room.

"Oh my Gosh, it's beautiful. Absolutely gorgeous. And the fireplace is the backside of the one in the Master right?" she asked.

"Yes you are, and yes, it's a two sided fireplace that goes from the master to the Master Bath," he said, enveloping her in an embrace.

"You never told me what you would you change about this place, if hypothetically of course, it was yours."

"Well," she said, taking another look around, "I think I'd change," turning to look directly at the man standing beside her, "absolutely nothing. This home has been designed as if someone had entered my mind and taken every sketch, dream and thought I've ever had for my dream home. I don't think there's a thing that I'd change about it and as I said before, I have a feeling that once my parents stay here for the weekend, you'll be hard pressed to get them to leave! And if you're insisting that my parents stay here, which I might add, was so incredibly thoughtful of you to make these arrangements for them; then I insist on at least paying the bill. And yes, I know we're about to become man and wife and it'll be our money, but I feel funny about you paying for my parents."

"Nic," he said cautiously, you don't have to pay me anything. I fell in love with this place the second I saw it and it screamed you, so I sort of put a deposit down on it to hold it until I could show it to you and if you like it, it's ours."

Watching her expression change, he suddenly panicked, not quite sure if he'd really screwed up this time or not.

Nicole heard what he had said, but couldn't quite believe what she was hearing. She looked at the man who was about to become her husband.

"You bought this house for me?"

"Actually, yes. From the day that I met you Nicole, everything I've done has been with you in mind. You fill my every waking moment and I would give my life and my last penny to make you happy. Don't you know that by now? I bought this thinking of you and thought that it would or could be a new start with you. That is if you'd like to put roots down here, in this town, running the clinic. It's not the pace you had at your hospital, nor is it the intensity I dealt with while in the military but we are still helping people and the people up here need us so I'm okay with a slower pace. And I figured if we're going to be working up here for a while, we might as well stay in something a little more comfortable while we're here."

"So technically, you bought this place without consulting with me? Is that correct?" she asked, without revealing what she was feeling at the moment.

"Um, I suppose, technically, yes I did. But actually, I told the agent that I'd like to purchase this place for my bride as a wedding present but added that if you didn't like it, I could get my deposit back."

She didn't respond, but pulled him into an embrace and as her lips met his, kissed him as if there was no tomorrow.

"I love it Aedan, and I love you. You make me so happy and if this home is where we are supposed to start the next chapter of our lives, and then I think we should go for it. I love this home from what I've seen so far, and know that we could put our signature on it and make it truly more amazing than what it already is."

"Really? Really, you love it" he asked in disbelief? You're okay with me picking out and buying our first home together?"

Thinking back to what she'd done to Jared when she'd found the home that was meant to be their first, she simply smiled at Aedan and answered his question. "Yes, yes I really love it and can't believe that you picked out something so amazing for us. And yes, I would love to start our new life here with you Aedan. That is, as long as Neiko is welcome too," she kidded.

"Neiko comes as part of the package. So yes, he's welcome as well."

"Then deal," she said, kissing him deeply and intensely. "Wanna see how comfortable that tub is Aedan?" she asked, with a wickedly provocative look on her face.

"As much as that sounds incredibly inviting Nic, your parents are planning on arriving tomorrow morning, so I think that we'd better get home and get ready for their arrival. They said that they'd be in by early afternoon so we had better head back, don't you think?"

Grabbing the back side of his jeans, she smiled a wickedly seductive smile.

"Suit yourself soldier. I can wait. Oh, and Aedan, when can we close on this place and move in? Because I intend to have you inside me, in that tub, in the very near future," she said as she moved her hand from the back of his jeans, to the front. Feeling every bit of restraint waning, he answered as the oxygen left his brain. "Soon Nic, really soon.

Chapter 48

They rode into work on the last day before their wedding, together, as usual. They were closing the clinic on Friday so that they could spend it with friends and family before the wedding. Even though it wasn't really a formal type affair, it was still a celebration and both needed to take time to look their best for the event. Danielle had taken half the week off and was working on the final details of how she wanted the town hall decorated for the post ceremony party. When Gwen and Jimmy arrived mid-day on Thursday, along with their daughter, had stopped by the clinic to say hello and check in. Everyone hugged and kissed and the increasing excitement could be felt in the air. Even Miranda and Deanna commented how excited they were to be attending the nuptials. But in typical melodramatic fashion, Miranda still remained glued to her news channel and on line sites pertaining to the increasing tension and stalemate that appeared to be happening between Alzatar and both the United States and Canada. The extremists associated with the government of Alzatar had stated that they'd changed the deadline to the 13th, which happened to be less than twenty-four hours away, and the day of Nicole's wedding. Neither she nor Danielle gave it any thought, thinking it was unique enough that they'd chosen Friday the 13th to exchange vows with the men in their lives. Both Bruce and Aedan had talked about their concerns in depth and both had varying levels of concern, but each kept that level to himself. Aedan had been in contact with several of his friends that were still active in the military and all had offered the same opinion; that Alzatar had the capability to evoke a chemical or EMP attack but no one that he'd spoken with felt that they had the balls or opportunity to stage a full blown attack and that the government would probably call their bluff, like they'd done with so many other nations, and that nothing would come of their empty threats. So he'd worry about tomorrow when tomorrow came.

"Aren't you worried about what could happen tomorrow Aedan?" Miranda asked, with her voice full of genuine concern.

"Sure I'm worried, Nicole might decide to not show up for the wedding," he joked.

"You know what I mean Aedan," she responded, trying to keep him on topic.

Now speaking in a serious and sincere tone, "yes Miranda, in all actuality, I am concerned about any organization, or nation that is threatening to do harm to our nation. I don't know if they can or will do anything tomorrow; and there is nothing more that we can do to change or prevent it so I guess we're forced to accept that whatever will be, will be."

With a semi-smile coming across her face, Miranda tried to put on a brave front, though inside, she had a very strong feeling of impending doom.

"I guess you're right Doc. So let's go get em' out there and wrap this day up as quickly as possible."

Putting his arm gently around his office manager, she gave her a sisterly hug. "Now that's the spirit. And away we go."

The day flew by and before they even had a chance to check the time, the last patient had been seen and was leaving. Nicole and Aedan promised to stay calm and get a good night's sleep, with both Deanna and Miranda offering last minute help should they need it. They made their way home and as they pulled into their drive, Nicole felt the hair on her arms rise and wasn't sure why but the second their home came into view, she knew the reason for her subconscious reaction. There, standing in the doorway of their temporary home were two of the most important people in their lives, and truth be told, probably the catalyst for the two of them becoming a couple. Alfred and Maria waved and stepped out of the doorway, with Neiko in tow to greet the future bride and groom. Nicole didn't know how they did it or how they knew about the wedding, but by the grin and full blown dimples radiating from Aedan's face, she quickly realized that he knew more than he was telling her. She'd deal with him later. But right now, she wanted nothing more than to give the people whom she considered her second parents, a huge hug. She ran toward them as they made their way toward her as well. The four met in the middle of the yard amongst laughter, smiles and tears. Neiko darted in and out of their legs as they embraced.

"Oh my god, I can't believe you're here! You're actually here."

With tears streaming down her face, she laughed and cried at the same time.

"You drove all this way just to come up and see us?" she asked, as she punched Aedan in the arm.

"And you knew they were coming and didn't tell me, you jackass!" she jested.

"Baby doll, we told you we'd come if you ever needed us," Maria said, as she held on to the young woman that she loved like her own daughter.

"And if your momma can't be here for you, well then, I told Drew that wild horses wouldn't keep me away," she said with a smile on her face and in her heart.

"We've missed you both so much and we were thrilled, but not surprised, when Aedan called, telling us the good news."

Looking at Aedan, she smiled. "Thank You Aedan."

"You're welcome my love. I just really thought that the people who forced us to see what was right in front of us should be present when we tie the knot."

"And I'm so glad that you did. Now let's all go inside and celebrate."

"Sounds like a plan."

Chapter 49

Nicole tossed and turned all night, having dream after dream and when she finally woke before dawn, unable to go back to sleep, she got up to make herself a cup of green tea to settle her nerves. She couldn't shake the uneasy feeling that she had, but also couldn't pinpoint what it was that was bothering her. Slipping on her robe, she made her way toward their kitchen, only to find Maria already up, ready to hand her a cup of green tea.

"Try this instead of your usual Earl Grey, it'll help."

Knowing that it was futile to even ask Maria how she knew that something was bothering her, she simply accepted the outstretched cup of tea and thanked her friend.

"I'm not sure what it is Maria, and today is supposed to be the happiest day of my life, but I know in my heart that something is not right and something is going to go wrong today. I just don't know what it is."

"You can't change destiny Nicole. What happens today is fate, whether it is created by man or by nature; it is meant to happen, whether we want it to or not. There is nothing that either you or I can do to stop it. I'm just glad we're all together."

"You feel it don't you Maria? And don't try to Bull Shit me. You have great insight and I know that you feel it as well don't you?"

"What I feel and what I see are two very different things. What I feel is that the world as we know it is very unsettled and there are many people who thrive on unrest. How our nation responds to them determines the final outcome of how we survive as a nation. What I see is a beautiful woman who's about to make an even more beautiful bride this evening, when she marries an amazing man. What I see is a man who has never loved the way he loves you, who never realized that he could give himself so freely, so completely, and feel so whole when he's in your presence. What happens today or anytime in the future for that matter, doesn't matter as long as you have family, friends, and someone to love. That philosophy is what has helped Andrew and I thrive all these years together, up in the boonies," she kidded. And you and Aedan will always be part of our family. And I," she said, reaching out to touch Nicole's hand, "cannot think of any place I'd rather be than here, right at this very moment. Any I want you to remember one thing Nicole; anytime, for whatever reason, always know that the door at the Lodge is open for you, Aedan and all of your family. And that invite extends to both your blood and adoptive families," she said, squeezing her hand.

"Thank you Maria. But I wish I knew why I'm so unsettled. Something is very off, and I even feel as if the air is off, you know what I mean. I just can't figure out what it is that's bothering me. Maybe it's just pre-ceremony jitters."

Not wanting to make her any more anxious than she already was, Maria smiled at her reassuringly, all the while knowing that Nicole's concerns were 100% founded. But as she'd stressed earlier; there was nothing that could be done to alter what may or may not happen, and Maria was just happy to be around people she loved, should her visions come to fruition.

After a light breakfast, Nicole excused herself and trying to maintain her usual routine, grabbed her dog's leash and took off for her morning run with Neiko. By the time she left, both Aedan and Andrew were up and Gwen and Danielle had already called, twice. Danielle sounded calm and collected, while Gwen sounded full of jitters. Nicole reassured Gwen that the day would be perfect and even the weather appeared to be cooperating as she looked out at the bright blue fall sky. Once on the road with her dog, they both got in sync with their rhythm and while Nicole sang along to the music emitting from her phone, Neiko kept stride at her side. She still felt unsettled but knew sticking to her usual routine would help soothe her nerves. Hoping that her family would make it in before noon, she kept the run relatively short. Her heart warmed at the thought that the man she loved; loved her so much that he went out and bought a home for her, for them; so that her parents and family could be comfortable while up visiting, and also so that they'd have a new home in which to start their new life. And the fact that he knew her so well that he'd picked out one that had everything she could possibly want in a home proved to her yet again, that she was making the right decision in giving marriage another shot. She rounded the corner of her long drive and screamed out loud seeing all the commotion in her front lawn. There, in front of her was her entire family, her parents, all of her brothers, their kids and their spouses. And in the middle of the mix was her future husband, and Andrew and Maria; the couple that had essentially become her second parents. Seeing everyone together made her realize just how wonderful her life was once again. But before she ran to see them, she couldn't help but look up at the cloudless sky and simply mouth the words "Thank You."

She truly felt blessed to have found love again, and to be loved by so many. And at that moment, all the worries that she'd woken up with that morning melted away as she ran to embrace her family.

Chapter 50

Even though it was an absolutely gorgeous morning, Miranda couldn't pull herself away from CNN and their continuing coverage of the passing of Alzatar's deadline for the release of their comrades and the threats that they were spewing since their demands hadn't been met by neither the United States nor the Canadian governments. Their masked representatives continued threat after veiled threat against both countries with the three nations appearing to be in a stalemate. So far, it appeared that their threats had been just that, propaganda. Miranda paced nervously as her boyfriend of three years tried to ignore her paranoia.

"You'll wear a hole in the carpet if you keep that shit up you know Miranda."

"Shut up will ya, this could be the beginning of the end as we know it, and you have nothing better to do than sit there and make fun of me?" she asked indignantly. "I don't want something bad to happen but damn it Clay, shit's about to hit the fan and you seem to think it's all a joke."

"Aw baby," he said, reaching for her, trying to appease her, "I know how much this stuff rattles you and no, I don't think it's a big joke. But at the end of the day love, you can't do jack shit about it except be prepared, which we are. And if the world goes crazy and all hell breaks loose, then we do what we've got to do to survive. Unfortunately, that's all we've got. But we're way ahead of most folks since we've been planning for the day, should it happen today, tomorrow, next month or next year. So for today, can we just forget about fucking Alzatar and their stupid threats and enjoy a day off together?" Winking, he added, "I know something we can do to make you forget all about Armageddon," he said, playfully slapping her rump.

Taking him up on his offer, Miranda shut off the TV literally five minutes before the news channels erupted with their breaking headlines.

Chapter 51

News spread fast over the internet compliments of sites like Facebook. All TV channels interrupted their regular broadcasts to disseminate whatever information they had and cell phones were jammed with people talking about the simultaneous attacks. Nobody thought that they'd had the ability to reach US soil, but within a matter of seconds, six major cities in the US and four cities in Canada had experienced total systems' failure shutdown. Chicago, Los Angeles, Atlanta, Washington, New York, Boston, Toronto, Montreal, Quebec City, and Vancouver all came to a halt when their computer systems all crashed simultaneously; with no one knowing the exact cause. It was quickly determined that EMP's were not to blame since not all computer systems failed; just the ones controlling every red light and crosswalk in the effected cities. All personal laptops within a certain radius, GPS systems and the main controls of the city's subway systems and total shutdown of traffic control at the various airports were also deemed useless. What was confusing to everyone involved was why only some computer systems went down, but not others. Cars were still running as people frantically tried to get back to their loved ones, and/or out of the cities. With no traffic control, it was inevitable that within a matter of minutes the car accidents were too numerous to count. Flights were being diverted because they couldn't land at the airports whose control towers were inoperable. Adding to the navigational nightmare, were distress signals coming in from numerous other commercial planes who all simultaneously received alerts, that their planes air supply had been tampered with and laced with an undisclosed chemical agent, thus adding to the panic in the skies.

What no one realized yet was that the group hadn't been plotting the attack for weeks as originally speculated, but had been organizing, orchestrating and strategizing their moves for years. For the last few decades, Alzatar had slowly been infiltrating not only into the big cities that were now on the brink of being crippled. But they had also integrated themselves into small towns across America and had been doing so for years. They'd slithered their families and their ways into the very towns where family values and our Nation's pride were the strongest. They'd raised their children to walk, talk, act like every other American child. They had their kids playing baseball beside all the other children in their small Mom and Pop towns, and all the while, they instilling and ingraining pure hatred for anyone who didn't hold their same beliefs, values and customs. They had so inconspicuously melted into society that no one had even noticed that the invasion was not taking place now; it had already happened years before. They'd taught their children to be "Americanized" during the day, and taught them how to be martyrs for their warped cause at night.

Now those very same people were using the children that they'd raised in those small towns to destroy those very same towns. Water supplies were contaminated, in some cases chemicals were released into water and in other towns, or the water supply had simply been depleted without anyone's knowledge. It hadn't taken but minutes to have pandemonium break out in big cities and small towns alike with everyone bracing for the next assault, thus adding to the panic that Alzatar was banking on.

Nicole, Aedan, Gwen and Jimmy were oblivious to what was happening throughout the country until they met up with Bruce and Danielle. Danielle knew that her internet had gone down but didn't really think anything of it since living up in the mountains, it was a common occurrence. It wasn't until Bruce returned from town that he updated her on the crisis unfolding around them. Danielle knew that all hell could potentially break out and people were so unpredictable when panic stricken but she honestly wasn't too worried about a few unorganized lone-wolf types of attacks. What she didn't know at the time was that they weren't a few so called martyrs carrying out the attacks, but were a very organized mass attack, all formulated and orchestrated by the same mastermind; and what had occurred so far was only the beginning of what was planned.

Even after Danielle's grim news, Nicole and Aedan went about the day visiting with family and friends. Aedan's on the other hand, tryied very hard to contain his nerves. As the afternoon made its' way toward evening and their impending nuptials, the three grooms left their brides-to-be and headed towards Aedan's future home, leaving the ladies amongst family to get ready. The air felt electric with happy tears and excitement, and Nicole's sister-in-law's fussing over all three brides equally. Even Gwen's parents were getting into a festive mood, though they were still slightly miffed at her for having a baby before wedlock; to which she got a big chuckle out of their whole antiquated outlook. The town hall had been decorated. The minister was dressed and ready, and all the guests were starting to make their way toward town and within the hour, Nicole and the other brides would become Mrs.' It was Nicole's mother, along with Maria that came to her room to tell her it was time to head into town. When the two older women took one look at Nicole, in her long billowy non-traditional wedding gown, she took their breathe away. She might not have wanted to look anything like a bride again, but standing there, with her hair flowing down over her shoulders with just a few strands bobby pinned back with baby's breathe intermingled; she looked not only stunning, but every bit a bride. Knowing that she was getting nervous just from her solemn expression, both women simply hugged her and told her how proud they were of her. And Maria being Maria, said what Nicole needed to hear.

"Jared would be so proud of you honey. He would never have wanted you to spend the rest of your life alone Nicole Rose. And I just know that he'll be right there with us today when you give yourself to Aedan; and in my heart I know that Jared will be smiling down on the two of you. So no tears baby girl. Let's get you to that ceremony!"

Nicole said nothing, but through the tears that she'd tried so desperately to will away, simply nodded in agreement. With both mother and surrogate mother at her side, she walked out of the cabin and toward the waiting car.

The lone hawk hovered overhead and tilted his wings, soaring toward town and the start of Nicole's new life.

Chapter 52

The town hall was completely full when the three brides arrived. Everyone was talking about, speculating on, predicting, and worrying about what was happening all around them. Both young and old offered opinions regarding what could possibly happen next, with faint paranoia intermingled amongst their conversations. Some felt that anyone new to an area should be ostracized, others had the "don't trust anybody" attitude, while others were ready to hole up in their bunkers and ride it out; just like they'd been prepping for all along. No one tried to change anyone's attitude, outlook or opinion, and the conversations continued incessantly until the town deacon came to the podium attempting to get everyone's attention.

As he looked out at the completely packed hall, he suddenly realized just how much of an impact both Danielle and Bruce, along with Nicole and Aedan had had on the town that he'd grown up in. Intermingled amongst Mystique River's residents were numerous families from Destiny, some of which even he had never met. Young and old, individuals and families, they had all been positively affected by Nicole and Aedan's presence.

Once everyone finally settled down and the hall was silent, he addressed what was on everyone's mind. Trying to reassure them, or at least offering them a false sense of security that in their remote, quiet area of New Hampshire, he suggested that no one would be interested in seeking them out, or causing them harm. He tried, unsuccessfully, to remind them that they were but a blip on the map and not exactly a huge metropolis or target for anyone. He got a few chuckles out of the people in attendance, and wishful nods, but deep down, he knew that most of the citizens of Mystique and Destiny wanted nothing more than to witness the ceremony and then get back to their own homes to wait out what was going to happen next. Just as he was about to signal the organist to start the procession march, a young teen who'd been glued to his I-phone yelled out "They've wiped out the white house! They bombed the white house!" Shrieks and gasps could be heard everywhere. Refusing to allow his hall to turn into a free-for-all of mass hysteria, the deacon silenced everyone demanding their attention. He bluntly told them that there was nothing that they could do for the people of Washington right now and at the moment, they had 6 people needing their attention. With that, he signaled the organist who was all too ready to start playing. Just as Nicole and Danielle had wanted, several of the town's children, accompanied by Nicole's nieces and nephews started down the make shift aisle towards the front of the hall. Each was dressed in attire of their choosing, and somehow the mismatched ensembles worked. As soon as the children started walking, everyone within the hall momentarily forgot about the outside world. As the children made their way forward, a few last minute guests slipped into the few empty chairs in the hall and were noticed by few.

Now it was the ladies' turn. As the men stood at the front of the hall, surrounded by children of every size and age, their eyes were glued to the back where Danielle was the first to appear, followed by Gwen, with Nicole bringing up the rear. Each bride looked uniquely different yet each looked equally beautiful. Their appearances were as varied as their personalities but each one made a statement, and each bride locked eyes on her man as she made her way down the aisle and to them. They now had everyone's attention as they joined their future husbands. Still on edge, the deacon maneuvered his way through the ceremony as quickly as he could, and before the clock tower outside stuck six, the ceremony was over. All three couples didn't hesitate when the deacon made his final announcement that they may kiss their respective bride, with the entire hall erupting in applause and a few scattered tears. Everyone within the four walls of the hall had momentarily forgotten about the insanity unfolding in their nation and their northern neighbors in Canada. As the couples turned to walk out of the hall to the continuing sound of applause, whistles and laughter, Bruce looked out into the audience for his mother. Making direct eye contact with her, he felt his heart nearly burst. Then he saw the woman who'd slid in beside her and even after all of these years, he'd know her anywhere, and couldn't believe his eyes. His aunt was here. His aunt was back.

"Arla?" he said, more to himself than to anyone in particular. Seeing him staring at her, she smiled, blowing him a kiss.

"Oh my God Danielle, it's my Aunt Arla; she's here. She's finally come home."

As he said the words to his new bride, Nicole and Gwen both heard what he said; and instantly Nicole felt the hair on her arms rise as she looked in the direction where Bruce's mother was standing, and she knew instantly. There, standing beside Moriah was the woman of her dreams, her prayers, and all of her wishes since she was a little girl.

"Momma?"

Gwen spoke up.

"Oh my God Nicki, is that your mother?"

Nicole didn't need confirmation. She simply said "Yes" and smiled as she saw the hawk outside the window tilt its' majestic wing and fly away.

Authors Note: Forgive me for leaving you hanging at the conclusion of Mystique River Justice. There are so many avenues I could have taken with their story, and even as I write this, I still have a multitude of scenarios swirling in my head. As much as I love my characters, Nicole & Aedan, Danielle & Bruce, Gwen & Jimmy; I feel that as a writer, there are still different genres of writing for me to explore. I don't know if this is the end of their story or not, but I can tell you that the next book I publish will be quite different from my previous stories. I don't want to reveal too much but I can tell you that it will be set completely within the Adirondack Park and the main character will be someone you either loathe or love; but she definitely will be one that you'll never forget! Don't judge her too quickly. She is completely different from our Nicole, but her story needs to be told as well....

~~~Erin Maine~~~

Made in the USA
Lexington, KY
18 January 2017